CORFU TRAVEL GUIDE 2024

From Pristine Beaches To Historic Sites, Experience The Best Of Corfu With Expert Insights

Ida E. Williams

No part of this book may be reproduced in any form or by any electronic or mechanical means, including information storage and retrieval systems, without permission in writing from the publisher, except by a reviewer who may quote brief passages in a review. This book is a work of non-fiction. The views and the opinions expressed in this book are the author's own and do not necessarily reflect those of the publisher or any other person or organization. The information in this book is provided for educational and informational purposes only. It is not intended as a substitute for professional advice of any kind.

Table of Contents

INTRODUCTION
Discover Corfu's Timeless Charm and History

History Unveiled

The lovely island of Corfu cradled in the turquoise embrace of the Ionian Sea, has captivated travelers for centuries with its rich history, vibrant culture, and breathtaking scenery. As we travel through time, let us delve into the fascinating tapestry of Corfu's past, where myth and fact weave together to form a gripping narrative.

Mythical Origins

Corfu, also known as Kerkira in Greek, is said to be named after the nymph Korkyra, who was kidnapped by the sea deity Pose idon and brought to the island as his bride. The union between mortal and divine gave rise to a realm of unprecedented splendor, endowed with lush greenery, beautiful waterways, and a climate that seems eternally kissed by the sun.

Ancient influences
Corfu's history is strongly entrenched in its strategic location at the crossroads of the Mediterranean, which attracted the interest of ancient civilizations looking to establish footholds in the region.

The island's first residents were the Phaeacians, a maritime people recorded in Homer's epic poem, The Odyssey.

Corfu's legendary monarch, Alcinous, is claimed to have welcomed the wandering hero Odysseus to his shores, contributing to the island's mythology.

Corfu's fate has been entwined with that of Greek city-states, the Roman Empire, and the Byzantine era, each leaving unmistakable marks on its environment and culture. The Venetians, with their nautical prowess, dominated the island for centuries, influencing its architecture, governance, and commerce. The classic Venetian fortifications that stand sentinel over Corfu Town, including the imposing Old Fortress and the elegant New Fortress, bear testament to this legacy of Venetian influence.

During the Renaissance and Enlightenment periods, Corfu was a beacon of intellectual and creative flowering, attracting scholars, philosophers, and painters from all across Europe. The Venetian nobility supported the arts, resulting in masterpieces of painting, sculpture, and literature that still grace the island's museums and galleries today.

The Ottoman Interlude and British Influence

Corfu was briefly under Ottoman authority in the 18th century before joining the British Empire in the early 19th century. The British period saw substantial improvements, such as infrastructure renovation, the introduction of English-style gardens, and the formation of a cosmopolitan culture that drew travelers, writers, and dignitaries from all over the world.

The Greek saga

The twentieth century was a turning point in Corfu's history, as it became a vital part of modern Greece. The island played a role in the resistance against Axis powers during World War II, and its post-war development saw a resurgence of tourism, marking the beginning of Corfu's reputation as a beloved destination for travelers seeking sun, sea, and culture.

Today's Corfu

Today, Corfu perfectly integrates its historic past with contemporary charm, providing visitors with a kaleidoscope of experiences ranging from visiting ancient ruins and Byzantine churches to relaxing on lovely beaches and relishing the tastes of its Mediterranean cuisine. The island's UNESCO-listed Old Town, with its winding lanes, Venetian houses, and hidden squares, invites visitors to travel back in time and discover the essence of Corfu's timeless charm. As we embark on this journey through Corfu's history, we invite you to immerse yourself in its tales of myth and legend, conquests and alliances, art and innovation. Let Corfu's past be your guide as you explore the present and create your memories on this captivating island in the heart of the Ionian Sea.

Embracing the Cultural Tapestry of Corfu

Ancient Heritage

Corfu's culture has its roots in its ancient occupants, which included Phaeacians, Greeks, Romans, and Byzantines. These civilizations bequeathed a legacy of art, architecture, and rituals that still influence the island's cultural landscape. From the remains of ancient temples and theaters to the intricate mosaics and frescoes found in archaeological sites, Corfu's ancient heritage is a treasure trove waiting to be explored.

Corfu's culture has been heavily influenced by Venetian sovereignty over the centuries.

The Venetians brought a passion for the arts, music, and literature, which thrived under their patronage. Corfu's towns and villages are known for their Venetian architecture, which features exquisite castles, fortresses, and churches with ornate façade and intricate decorations. Corfu's culinary culture also reflects the Venetian influence, with dishes that combine Italian and Greek flavors to produce a one-of-a-kind gastronomical experience.

British Influence
The British period in Corfu's history had an indelible impact on its culture, particularly in administration, education, and social norms. The British introduced modern infrastructure, including roads, schools, and hospitals, which paved the way for Corfu's development in the 19th and 20th centuries. English gardens became popular, and the tradition of afternoon tea took root, adding a touch of British elegance to the island's lifestyle.

Mediterranean Melting Pot
Corfu's strategic location in the Mediterranean has resulted in a melting pot of civilizations and influences. Over the years, the island has welcomed traders, sailors, and tourists from all across Europe and the Middle East, adding to its complex tapestry of traditions, dialects, and beliefs. Corfu's festivals highlight its cultural richness by combining music,

dancing, and cuisine from several regions in a harmonic synthesis.

Art and Architecture

Venetian Splendor

Corfu's art and architecture reached their peak during the Venetian period, which lasted from the 14th to the 18th century. The Venetians brought skilled craftsmen and painters to the island, resulting in masterpieces that decorated churches, castles, and public areas. The recognizable Venetian strongholds, including the Old Fortress overlooking Corfu Town and the coastal fortifications, showcase the architectural prowess of this era.

Byzantine treasures

Corfu's Byzantine legacy is visible in its churches and monasteries, which contain precious icons, paintings, and religious relics. The Church of Saint Spyridon, with its silver reliquary carrying the remains of the island's patron saint, is a pilgrimage site revered by locals and visitors alike. The Paleokastritsa Monastery, set on a rock overlooking the sea, is another Byzantine-influenced architectural masterpiece.

Music & Dance

Folk Traditions

Corfu's folk music and dance traditions are strongly ingrained in its rural areas, where songs and dances are passed down through the centuries. Clarinet, violin, and accordion music fill village squares during festivals and celebrations, accompanied by energetic dances such as the "Syrtos" and "kalamatianos."These traditional performances highlight island's cultural heritage and bring communities together in joyful expression.

Ionian Serenades

The musical tradition of the Ionian Islands, which includes Corfu, is recognized for its melodic richness and poetic lyrics. The "cantades," or serenades, are a popular style of musical storytelling in which singers narrate stories of love, desire, and nostalgia accompanied by guitars and mandolins. These serenades are an important aspect of Corfu's cultural identity, creating feelings that resonate with both locals and visitors.

Cuisine & Gastronomy

Mediterranean Flavors

Corfu's food celebrates fresh ingredients, robust flavors, and centuries-old culinary traditions. Corfiot cuisine is a beautiful blend of land and sea, with an emphasis on olive oil, herbs, seafood, and local products. From savory soups to barbecued meats to seafood meze and sweet pastries, Corfu's gastronomy is a journey of taste and discovery.

Local Delicacies

Corfu's must-try dishes include "pastitsada," a savory pasta dish with spiced meat sauce; "sofrito," thinly sliced beef cooked in a white wine and garlic sauce; and "bourdeto," a spicy fish stew with Mediterranean tastes. Corfu's seaside cuisine is based on freshly caught seafood, such as octopus, squid, and red mullet, which is frequently grilled or marinated in herbs and olive oil.

Festivals and Celebrations

Easter Traditions

Easter is a time for lively celebration in Corfu, with religious processions, feasts, and cultural events. The practice of "pot throwing" on Holy Saturday, in which inhabitants throw clay pots from their balconies, represents the renewal of life and the breaking of old habits. The resurrection ceremony on Easter Sunday at midnight is a light and music show, with rockets lighting up the night sky and bands playing traditional melodies.

Summer Festivals

Summer brings a rush of festivals and cultural events to Corfu, presenting local and international performers in music, dance, theater, and the arts. The Corfu Festival, held in several venues throughout the island, comprises classical concerts, opera performances, and ballet productions that draw visitors from all over the world. The "Dukas" festival in the village of Peroulades commemorates traditional Corfiot music and dancing, and guests are welcome to participate.

Language & Literature

Ionian Poetry

Corfu has a strong literary past, molded by its Ionian heritage and the many cultural influences that have shaped the island's identity. Dionysios Solomos, a Corfu native and Greek national poet, exemplifies the romanticism and idealism of the Ionian school of poetry. Solomos' epic poetry "Hymn to Liberty," which inspired the Greek national anthem, is a testament to Corfu's role in the struggle for independence.

Linguistic Legacy

Corfu's language is a combination of Greek, Italian, and Venetian dialects known as "Corfiot Greek." This language diversity is reflected in ordinary discussions, local expressions, and folk tunes, which highlight the island's cultural richness. The preservation of native language and dialects demonstrates Corfu's commitment to preserving its past and identity.

Discover Corfu's Geographic Wonders and Climate Charms

A land of natural splendor

Corfu, nestled in the Ionian Sea, entices visitors with its various landscapes, which range from lush foliage and golden beaches to craggy mountains and azure waters. On our voyage to discover Corfu's geographic beauties, we will learn about the island's topology, wildlife, and the wonderful interplay of land and water.

Geographical Overview

Location and Size

Corfu, located off the west coast of Greece measures around 64 kilometers long and 32 kilometers wide, with a total area of 592 square kilometers. Its strategic location near the Adriatic Sea and the Albanian coast has influenced its history and culture for ages.

Topography

Corfu's topography is diverse, ranging from coastal plains to mountainous highlands. The island's eastern coast is rather flat, with sandy beaches and rich plains suitable for cultivation. In contrast, the western and northern areas of Corfu are mountainous, with peaks rising beyond 900 meters and providing panoramic views of the sea and adjacent islands.

Coastal Beauty

Corfu's coastline is a tapestry of sandy beaches, secret coves, and cliffs that create breathtaking views around the coast. Some of the most famous beaches include Paleokastritsa, with its blue waves and lush green backdrop; Glyfada, with its golden sands and water sports activities; and Sidari, which is home to the unique rock formations known as the "Canal d'Amour."

Inland Delights

Inland, Corfu shows a panorama of olive trees, vineyards, and citrus orchards that thrive in the Mediterranean climate. Picturesque villages dot the landscape, each with its own unique charm and traditional architecture. The interior of the island is a sanctuary for nature enthusiasts, with hiking routes leading to waterfalls, caverns, and panoramic views of the sea.

Climate & Weather

Corfu's Mediterranean environment, with moderate winters and hot, dry summers, makes it an ideal year-round tourism destination. The island has four distinct seasons, each with its allure and opportunity for outdoor recreation.

Spring (March-May)

Corfu's springtime is a color symphony, with wildflowers blooming and the landscape coming to life with brilliant hues. The temperature ranges from 15°C to 20°C (59°F to 68°F), making it ideal for hiking, seeing historic sites, and enjoying outdoor eating with fresh seasonal produce.

Summer (June–August)

Summer is Corfu's busiest tourist season, with long sunny days and temperatures ranging from 25°C to 35°C (77°F to 95°F). Sunseekers are drawn to the beaches, while water sports fans can participate in activities such as snorkeling, diving, or sailing.

Evenings are filled with bustling tavernas, music festivals, and cultural activities celebrating the island's heritage.

Autumn (September–November)

Autumn brings a mild transition as temperatures gradually fall, ranging from 20°C to 25°C (68°F to 77°F).

It's the ideal time to explore Corfu's countryside, visit wineries during the grape harvest season, and attend traditional harvest festivities.

The sea is still warm, inviting swimmers to enjoy their final days of beach enjoyment.

Winter (December – February)

Corfu's winter is moderate in comparison to northern Europe, with average temperatures ranging from 10°C to 15°C (50°F to 59°F). While the island receives periodic showers, it also provides a tranquil setting for nature excursions, viewing historic monuments without crowds, and dining at quaint tavernas providing hearty local food.

Climate Variability

Corfu's microclimates provide an intriguing depth to its weather patterns. The eastern shore is generally dryer and sunnier, making it excellent for beachgoers and water sports aficionados. In contrast, the western and northern regions receive more rainfall, which results in lush flora and fertile valleys for agriculture.

Biodiversity And Nature Reserves

Flora and Fauna

Corfu has a great biodiversity due to its diverse terrain and good climate. Olive trees, cypress, and citrus fruits thrive in the fertile soil, while aromatic herbs such as oregano, thyme, and rosemary perfume the air. The island is also home to a diverse array of wildlife, including birds of prey, migratory birds, and marine species along its coastline.

Natural Reserves

Several natural reserves and protected places demonstrate Corfu's commitment to environmental preservation. The Pantokrator Mountain Range, with its lush woods and hiking trails, is a Natura 2000 site that protects indigenous flora and species. The wetlands of Lake Korission and Antinioti Lagoon provide crucial habitat for migratory birds and endangered species.

Human Geography and Cultural Landmarks

Corfu Town

Corfu's capital, Corfu Town (Kerkyra), is a UNESCO World Heritage Site known for its Venetian, French, and British architectural influences. The Old Town's tiny alleyways, colorful facades, and historic buildings, such as the Liston Promenade and the Palace of St. Michael and St. George, reflect centuries of cultural interaction and artistic expression.

Villages and Traditions

Beyond Corfu Town, the island's villages provide insight into traditional life and customs.

From the stone-built settlements of Pelekas and Benitses to the fishing villages of Kassiopi and Agios Stefanos, each location tells a unique tale through local crafts, festivals, and culinary traditions. The yearly Easter celebrations, complete with religious processions and cultural customs, emphasize Corfu's long-standing traditions.

Historical Landmarks

Corfu's cultural environment is peppered with ancient landmarks that reflect the island's rich heritage. Empress Elisabeth of Austria erected the Achilleion Palace, which exemplifies neoclassical architecture and imperial magnificence. The Mon Repos Estate, formerly a summer home for Greek nobility, is surrounded by exquisite gardens and ancient artifacts that offer insights into the island's past.

Conclusion

As we wrap up our tour of Corfu's geography and climate, we're reminded of the island's incredible diversity and natural beauty. Corfu, with its mountainous landscapes and gorgeous beaches, as well as its vibrant cultural legacy and welcoming climate, provides a holistic experience that captivates visitors and leaves a lasting impression. Whether sunbathing in the Mediterranean sun, visiting ancient ruins, or relishing local food, Corfu welcomes tourists to immerse themselves in a tapestry of geographic beauties and climate charms that characterize its own identity in the Ionian Sea.

Discovering the Fascinating World of Corfu

As we continue on our trip to uncover the beauties of Corfu, let's look at some intriguing and lesser-known facts that add to the island's attraction.

1. Mythological Origins

Corfu's name is rooted in mythology, dating back to the Nymph Korkyra, who was supposed to be the daughter of the river deity Asopos. Legend says that Poseidon, the god of the sea, fell in love with Korkyra and carried her to the island, where they founded a city and named it after her. This mythical tale adds a touch of romance and mystique to Corfu's identity, as it is believed to be named after a divine figure from ancient Greek mythology.

2. Venetian Legacy

Corfu's centuries-long link with the Venetian Republic has had a significant impact on its history. Corfu was ruled by the Venetians from the 14th century to the late 18th century, and their influence on its architecture, culture, and traditions is still felt today. The distinctive Venetian fortresses that dominate the terrain, particularly the Old Fortress and the New

Fortress in Corfu Town, remain as permanent monuments of this Venetian history.

3. Olive Oil Capital

Corfu is well known for its high-quality olive oil, which has been produced on the island for centuries. The olive tree represents prosperity and serenity in Greek culture, and Corfu's olive gardens produce some of the best olive oil in the Mediterranean. Visitors can experience olive oil mills, sample freshly pressed oil, and learn about the ancient art of olive cultivation that has sustained Corfu's economy for generations.

4. Cultural Melting Pot

Corfu's strategic location at the crossroads of Europe and the Middle East has resulted in a cultural melting pot with influences from Greek, Italian, Ottoman, and British traditions. This cultural diversity is mirrored in the island's cuisine, music, language, and customs, resulting in a distinct tapestry of cultural legacy that still thrives today.

5. The Durrells' Island

Corfu rose to literary prominence as the setting for British novelist Gerald Durrell's autobiographical novel "My Family and Other Animals." The book covers Durrell's boyhood adventures on the island throughout the 1930s, capturing the grandeur of Corfu's natural surroundings and the eccentricity of its inhabitants. Durrell's fascinating stories drew international attention to Corfu as a literary and cultural sanctuary.

6. UNESCO World Heritage

Corfu's Old Town, with its convoluted lanes, antique buildings, and Venetian castles, is a UNESCO World Heritage site. The Old Town's well-preserved medieval architecture, which includes the Liston Promenade, Spianada Square, and the Church of Saint Spyridon, provides insight into the island's history and cultural significance in the Mediterranean region.

7. Musical Traditions

Corfu has a rich musical past, including classic genres like "kantades" (serenades) and "corfuiko" (Corfiot music), which reflect the island's cultural roots. The sounds of mandolins, guitars, and clarinets fill the air during festivals and festivities, where both locals and visitors congregate to enjoy colorful music and dance performances that capture the essence of Corfu's dynamic culture.

8. The Easter Pot-Throwing Tradition

One of Corfu's most distinctive customs is the "Botides" or "Pot Throwing" ritual, which is observed on Holy Saturday during Easter celebrations. Residents toss ceramic pots from their balconies, resulting in a cacophony of crashing pottery that represents fresh life and the breaking of old patterns. This colorful and festive tradition attracts spectators from far and wide, adding a touch of whimsy to Corfu's Easter festivities.

9. British Influence
Corfu was under British authority in the nineteenth century, which had a long-term impact on its infrastructure, education, and social practices. The British established contemporary amenities including roads, schools, and gardens, influencing Corfu's development and establishing a cosmopolitan culture that drew visitors and dignitaries from all over the world. British influence may still be observed in Corfu's architecture, tea culture, and historical sites.

10. Saint Spyridon's Home
Corfu is home to the relics of Saint Spyridon, the island's patron saint and a venerated figure in Orthodox Christianity. The Saint Spyridon Church in Corfu Town houses the saint's bones in a silver reliquary, which is paraded through the streets during religious processions and festivals. Pilgrims and believers go to the church to honor Saint Spyridon and seek his blessings on health and prosperity.

11. Filming location for films and television shows
Corfu's beautiful scenery and old architecture have made it a favorite filming destination for movies and television series.

The gorgeous villages, beaches, and landmarks of the island have been featured in films such as "The Greek Tycoon" and "For Your Eyes Only," as well as in the popular TV series "The Durrells," bringing Corfu's beauty to a global audience.

12. Fortresses and Castles
Corfu is home to several spectacular strongholds and castles, reflecting the island's strategic importance throughout history. The Old Fortress, erected by the Venetians in the 15th century, dominates Corfu Town and provides panoramic views of the sea and other islands. The Angelokastro Castle, built on a cliff in the northern portion of the island, offers an insight into Corfu's ancient defenses as well as panoramic views of the shoreline.

13. A Diverse Flora And Fauna
Corfu's various ecosystems sustain a wide range of flora and fauna, making it a haven for environment and wildlife aficionados. Migrant birds, butterflies, and small mammals call the island's olive groves, cypress trees, and citrus plantations home. Marine life thrives along Corfu's coastline, with dolphins, sea turtles, and colorful fish inhabiting its crystal-clear waters.

14. Wine and Gastronomy
Corfu's culinary scene is a feast for the senses, with traditional delicacies reflecting the island's cultural

past and agricultural riches. Local delicacies include "pastitsada" (pasta with spiced meat sauce), "bourdeto" (hot fish stew), and "sofrito" (beef cooked in wine and garlic sauce). Corfu's vineyards produce a range of wines, including the well-known "retsina" and "moschato," which complement the island's rich food.

15. Cosmopolitan Charm

Despite its tiny size, Corfu exudes a cosmopolitan atmosphere that draws people from all walks of life. The island's dynamic nightlife, beach resorts, and cultural events cater to a wide range of preferences, ensuring that everyone has something to enjoy. Whether visiting ancient ruins, lounging on sandy beaches, or savoring local specialties, Corfu welcomes visitors to immerse themselves in its rich tapestry of history, culture, and natural beauty.

CHAPTER ONE

Travel Essentials: Visa and Entry Requirements for Corfu, Greece

Many people dream of visiting Corfu, Greece, because of the breathtaking scenery, rich history, and active culture. However, before going on your adventure to this wonderful island, you must first grasp the visa and entry procedures to have a smooth and hassle-free vacation. In this detailed guide, we'll go over all you need to know about getting a visa, entrance permits, travel paperwork, and other important details for visiting Corfu.

Visa requirements
Schengen Zone Membership
Greece, including Corfu, is a member of the Schengen Zone, which provides for visa-free travel between

participating countries for brief visits. Visitors from certain countries, known as Schengen Visa Exempt Countries, do not need a visa to enter Greece for leisure or business purposes for stays of up to 90 days within 180 days.

Schengen Visa Requirements
If you are not a citizen of a Schengen Visa Exempt Country, you must apply for a Schengen Visa(Type C) before visiting Greece, including Corfu.
The Schengen Visa permits for stays of up to 90 days within 180 days and is valid for tourist, business, or family trips.

To apply for a Schengen Visa, please send the following documents to the Greek embassy or consulate in your country:

1. Completed Schengen visa application form.
2. Ensure your passport is valid for at least three months beyond your intended stay in Greece.
3. Recent passport-sized photos.
4. Travel itinerary with flight and accommodation details.
5. Provide proof of travel insurance with a minimum coverage of €30,000 for medical emergencies and repatriation.

6. Proof of financial means to fund your stay in Greece, such as bank statements, sponsorship letters, or credit card statements

7. Letter of Invitation (if applicable)

8. Provide proof of accommodation in Greece, such as hotel reservations or a letter from the host.

9. Demonstrate ties to your nation through job or education.

Visa-Free Entry For Specific Nationalities

Certain countries' citizens can enter Greece without a visa for short periods. These countries include EU member states, EEA (European Economic Area) countries, Switzerland, and certain non-EU countries that have visa waiver arrangements with Greece. Travelers from these countries are permitted to enter Greece and remain for up to 90 days within 180 days without a visa.

Extended Stay Visa (Type D)

An Extended Stay Visa (Type D) is necessary for those who intend to stay in Greece for more than 90 days, including on Corfu. This visa is valid for job, study, or family reunification and must be secured before arriving in Greece. The application process for an Extended Stay Visa involves additional documentation and requirements specific to the purpose of your stay.

Entry Requirements:

1. Valid passport

All visitors to Greece, including Corfu, must hold a valid passport. The passport must be valid for at least three months after the scheduled departure from Greece. To minimize problems during your vacation, verify your passport's expiration date well ahead of time and renew it if necessary.

2. Entry Stamp

When travelers arrive in Greece, Greek immigration officers will stamp their passports. This entry stamp shows the date of admission and the permitted length of stay, which is normally up to 90 days for tourists from Schengen Visa Exempt Countries. It is critical to check the entry stamp for accuracy and conformity with the permissible stay period.

3. Travel Documents

In addition to a valid passport and visa (if required), tourists
should carry these essential travel documents when visiting Corfu:

1. Provide a printed copy of your flight itinerary, including return or onward travel arrangements.
2. Confirmation of Corfu accommodation, including hotel reservations or rental agreements.

3. Travel insurance policy with coverage for medical emergencies, trip cancellation, and lost or stolen belongings
4. Contact information for your embassy or consulate in Greece
5. Provide a copy of your visa (if applicable) and any supporting documentation produced during the visa application process.
6. International driving permit (for car rentals in Corfu).

4. Health and Safety Requirements

When visiting Corfu, travelers may be required to meet health and safety criteria as part of their admission requirements.

1. Stay informed about current COVID-19 protocols in Greece and Corfu. This could include requirements for COVID-19 testing, immunization certificates, quarantine procedures, and mask mandates. Before visiting, make sure to check the most recent government updates.

2. Some nations may need proof of COVID-19 vaccination for entrance. Make sure to carry your immunization certificate or digital vaccination record if applicable.

3. Travel insurance that covers COVID-19 medical expenses is highly recommended. Check your insurance policy for details on pandemics and epidemics.

4. Health Declaration papers: Upon arriving in Greece, travelers may need to fill out health declaration papers and give health information. These forms may include questions regarding recent travel history, health symptoms, and contact information.

Customs and Immigration Procedures

When arriving in Corfu, visitors must go through customs and immigration processes at the port of entry, which is usually Corfu Foreign Airport (Ioannis Kapodistrias Airport) for foreign flights. Here are some key points about customs and immigration.

1. Customs Declaration: Upon arrival, you may need to fill out a customs declaration form to declare any valuable objects, cash amounts exceeding limits, and commodities subject to customs restrictions.
2. Bag Inspection: Customs authorities may inspect your bags. Prepare to provide receipts for valuable things and declare any restricted or prohibited goods.
3. Immigration Check: Show your passport, visa (if applicable), and entrance stamp to immigration agents for verification. Answer any questions about the purpose and duration of your stay in Corfu.
4. Visa Extension: To prolong your stay in Greece or modify your visa status (e.g., from tourist to student), apply through Greek immigration authorities.

Conclusion

Understanding the visa and entry criteria for traveling to Corfu, Greece, is critical for a successful and pleasurable trip. Whether you are a citizen of a Schengen Visa Exempt Country, need a Schengen Visa, or intend to stay in Greece for an extended period, following the criteria described in this guide will help you comply with legislation and have a stress-free travel experience. Remember to verify official sources and speak with relevant authorities or your travel agent for the most recent information.

Currency & Money Matters in Corfu, Greece

To ensure a successful and hassle-free trip to the picturesque Greek island of Corfu, you must first grasp the currency, banking services, payment methods, and money management recommendations. In this detailed guide, we'll go over everything you need to know about currency, money exchange, credit card uses, and financial management during your trip to Corfu.

Currency in Corfu

Euro (€) - Official Currency

Greece's national currency, including Corfu, is the euro (€). The Euro is divided into coin (cent) and banknote denominations, making it convenient for routine transactions. The coins come in denominations of one, two, five, ten, twenty, and fifty cents, as well as one & two euros. Banknotes come in values of 5, 10, 20, 50, 100, 200, and 500 Euros.

Currency code: EUR
The Euro's currency code is EUR, and it is utilized in financial transactions, currency exchange rates, and international banking operations. When dealing with currency exchanges or making payments in Corfu, you may encounter prices and amounts indicated in Euros (EUR).

Currency symbol: €.
The currency symbol for the Euro is €, which is well-known and used in pricing, billing, and displaying currency amounts. The Euro sign is used on banknotes, coins, and financial documents to represent Euro quantities.

Money-Management Tips

1. Currency Exchange
Before traveling to Corfu, it is important to exchange some currency into Euros so that you have cash on hand for initial needs upon arrival. Corfu's airports, banks, exchange offices (kiosks), and hotels all offer currency exchange services.

Compare exchange rates and fees to find the best deal when converting your currencies to Euros.

2. ATM Access

Corfu has a network of ATMs (Automated Teller Machines)
where you can withdraw euros with your debit or credit card. ATMs are found in major cities, tourist locations, and near banks. Before using an ATM in Corfu, check with your bank or card issuer about international ATM withdrawal fees, foreign transaction fees, and daily withdrawal limits before using ATMs in Corfu.

3. Credit Cards

Corfu's hotels, restaurants, stores, and tourist sites accept major credit cards including Visa, MasterCard, and American Express. Using credit cards for payments is convenient and secure, but be cautious of foreign transaction fees, currency conversion charges, and merchant acceptance regulations. Inform your card issuer of your trip plans to avoid card authorization complications while overseas.

4. Travel Checks

While traveler's checks were formerly a popular form of cash for international travel, their use has declined due to the widespread availability of ATMs and credit cards.

If you prefer traveler's checks for increased security, make sure they are issued in Euros and can be cashed easily at Corfu's banks and exchange offices.

5. Cash vs. Cards

For flexibility and convenience, it is advisable to carry both cash and credit cards. Use cash for minor purchases, local markets, and transactions where credit cards may not be accepted. Reserve cards are used for larger payments, hotel reservations, and online shopping.

Maintain a record of all transactions and receipts for budgeting and accounting purposes.

6. Currency Conversion applications

Download applications or use online converters to check exchange rates, convert currencies, and track expenses in Euros. These resources can assist you in making informed decisions about currency exchange, budgeting, and financial management while visiting Corfu.

7. Emergency Funds

Carry emergency funds in Euros or a backup payment method, such as a second credit card or prepaid travel card, in case of unexpected expenses, loss of wallet, or card issues. Keep emergency contact numbers for your bank, card issuer, and embassy handy for assistance with financial matters abroad.

Currency Exchange and Banking Services

Banks and Exchange Offices

Banks in Corfu provide currency exchange services, ATM access, and financial facilities to visitors. Major banks include *the National Bank of Greece, Alpha Bank, Piraeus Bank, and Eurobank Ergasias.* Currency exchange and cash withdrawals are also possible at exchange offices (kiosks) located in tourist destinations, airports, and ferry terminals.

Exchange Rates

Exchange rates for converting money to Euros can vary depending on the provider, location, and transaction method. Banks normally provide competitive exchange rates, whereas exchange offices may charge fees or commissions. Before exchanging money, compare rates and costs by checking exchange rates online or using currency converters.

ATM Withdrawals

ATMs on Corfu allow you to withdraw Euros using your debit or credit card with a PIN (Personal Identification Number). Check ATM locations, operating hours, withdrawal limits, and fees charged by your card issuer or bank for international transactions. Notify your bank about your travel plans to avoid card authorization issues abroad.

Bank Hours

Banking hours in Corfu vary by location and may be reduced on weekends, holidays, and siesta times. Most banks are open Monday through Friday, from 8:00 a.m. to 2:00 p.m., with some branches providing additional hours or afternoon sessions. In tourist locations, exchange offices and ATMs may operate 24 hours a day, seven days a week.

Payment Methods and Acceptance

Cash Payments

Cash is generally accepted in Corfu, particularly for modest purchases, dining at local tavernas, buying at markets, and paying for transportation. Carry tiny Euro denominations for convenience and to avoid dealing with change. Check for counterfeit notes and keep cash secure during transactions.

Credit and Debit Cards

Credit and debit cards are widely accepted in Corfu's hotels, restaurants, stores, rental car agencies, and tourist attractions. Visa and MasterCard are commonly utilized, followed by American Express and other credit card networks. To avoid dynamic currency conversion (DCC) costs, inform shops about the currency on your card (Euros).

Contactless Payments

Contactless payments using credit cards, mobile wallets (e.g., Apple Pay, Google Pay), and contactless-enabled devices are becoming more common in Corfu. Look for contactless payment symbols (such as the contactless card logo or the NFC emblem) at POS terminals to swiftly and securely touch and pay for items.

Online Payments

Credit cards are the most often used payment option for online bookings, reservations, and purchases. Make sure that the website is safe (https://) and employs encryption for online transactions. Verify billing information, currency conversions, and payment confirmation emails to ensure correctness and security.

Traveler's Checks

Traveler's checks are less often utilized. However, some Corfu banks and exchange offices may accept them for currency exchange or cash. Before utilizing traveler's checks as a payment option, verify their acceptance, fees, and exchange rates.

Currency Conversion and Exchange Rates

Real-time Exchange Rates

Using financial websites, currency converters, or mobile apps, you can monitor real-time Euro (EUR) exchange rates against your local currency. Exchange rates fluctuate according to market conditions, economic considerations, and geopolitical events, which affect the value of your currency when converting to Euros.

Exchange Rate Factors
Interest rates, inflation rates, political stability, economic indicators, market mood, and global events all have an impact on currency exchange rates. When converting money to euros, keep track of currency trends, rate movements, and the potential influence on your vacation budget.

Dynamic Currency Conversion (DCC)
When utilizing credit cards to make foreign currency payments, keep in mind that retailers may offer Dynamic Currency Conversion (DCC). DCC allows you to pay in your home currency (e.g., USD) rather than Euros (EUR), but it may result in higher exchange rates and costs. Choose to pay in Euros to avoid DCC fees and obtain better exchange rates.

Currency Converter Tools
Currency converter tools, applications, and online calculators can help you convert currency values, estimate expenditures, and manage expenses in Euros. These tools provide up-to-date exchange rates,

historical data, and conversion options for managing your travel budget effectively.

Conclusion

Understanding currency and financial issues is critical for a successful and pleasurable vacation to Corfu, Greece. Whether you're converting currency, using credit cards, withdrawing cash, or managing expenses, these ideas and guidelines can help you negotiate financial transactions, save money on fees, and make the most of your travel budget. Enjoy your stay in Corfu, immerse yourself in its beauty and culture, and create lasting memories on this intriguing island.

Language And Communication in Corfu, Greece

Understanding the local language, communication options, cultural subtleties, and helpful phrases will enrich your travel experience and facilitate interactions with locals as you embark on a journey to the lovely island of Corfu, Greece. In this comprehensive book, we'll go over everything you need to know about language basics, communication skills, and cultural insights for navigating Corfu with ease and confidence.

Language of Corfu

Greek (Official language)
Greece's official language, including Corfu, is Greek. Greek is a beautiful and musical language with a long history, several dialects, and distinctive linguistic features. While English is widely spoken in tourist areas, understanding a few basic Greek words can help you engage with locals and show respect for their culture.

Common Dialects
In addition to Standard Modern Greek, you may come across regional dialects and variations in Corfu. The Corfiot dialect, known as "Kerkyraiko," has Venetian, Italian, and English elements as a result of the island's historical connections and cultural interactions. Locals appreciate attempts to learn and employ regional idioms in conversation.

English Proficiency
English is commonly understood and spoken throughout Corfu's tourist districts, hotels, restaurants, stores, and attractions. Many locals, particularly those working in hospitality and tourism, speak English fluently and can easily communicate with guests. However, learning a few Greek phrases might help you enrich your cultural experience and connect with people on a deeper level.

Communication Tools and Tips

Basic Greek Phrases

Learning a few basic Greek phrases can be invaluable for communication and cultural immersion in Corfu. Here are some essential phrases to know:

1. **Hello / Goodbye:**
   - English: Hello / Goodbye
   - Greek: Γεια σας (Yia sas) / Αντίο (Adio)

2. **Thank you:**
   - English: Thank you
   - Greek: Ευχαριστώ (Efharisto)

3. **Please:**
   - English: Please
   - Greek: Παρακαλώ (Parakalo)

4. **Yes / No:**
   - English: Yes / No
   - Greek: Ναι (Ne) / Όχι (Ochi)

5. **Excuse me / Sorry:**
   - English: Excuse me / Sorry
   - Greek: Συγνώμη (Signomi) / Λυπάμαι (Lypamai)

6. **Do you speak English?:**
   - English: Do you speak English?

- Greek: Μιλάτε αγγλικά; (Milate agglika?)

7. **Where is...?:**
   - English: Where is...?
   - Greek: Πού είναι...; (Pou einai...?)

8. **How much is this?:**
   - English: How much is this?
   - Greek: Πόσο κοστίζει αυτό; (Poso kostizei afto?)

Language Apps and Resources

Use language learning apps, websites, and tools to improve your Greek language abilities before and during your visit to Corfu. Apps such as Duolingo, Babbel, and Memrise provide interactive lessons, vocabulary practice, and pronunciation guides. Carry a pocket phrasebook or use internet translation services for rapid reference.

Bilingual Signage

In tourist locations, signage, menus, and information boards are frequently bilingual, displaying both Greek and English. Look for English translations on street signs, public transit timetables, and tourist attractions to help you traverse Corfu more easily. Learn the Greek alphabet letters so you can recognize words and location names.

Cultural sensitivity

Respect Greek culture and customs by learning about local etiquette, greetings, and gestures. Greeks place a high priority on politeness, hospitality, and personal relationships throughout exchanges. Use formal greetings (e.g., "Yia sas") when meeting elders or in formal settings. Avoid using hand gestures that may be considered offensive or rude.

Communication Channels

1. English-Speaking Services

Corfu has many services for English-speaking guests, such as hotels, restaurants, tour operators, and information centers. Employees at tourist attractions frequently speak English effectively and may assist with inquiries, bookings, and recommendations. If you require assistance or explanation, please do not hesitate to ask.

2. Tourist Information Offices

Corfu tourist information offices, such as the Corfu Tourist Information Center, provide maps, brochures, event schedules, and local insights. The staff at these offices is knowledgeable about sites, activities, transportation alternatives, and cultural events, making them great resources for visitors.

3. Hotel concierge

If you are staying at a hotel in Corfu, the concierge desk
can help you with reservations, transportation, sightseeing tours, and eating recommendations. Make your preferences and needs clear to the concierge for personalized service and a memorable stay on the island.

4. Local Guides and Tours

Consider scheduling guided tours or hiring local guides in Corfu to discover historical sights, cultural landmarks, and natural wonders. Professional guides provide educational commentary, insider recommendations, and English language support to help you understand and enjoy the destination.

5. Mobile Apps and Online Services

Download travel apps and use online services for communication, navigation, and trip planning on Corfu. Language translation, offline maps, user ratings, and travel suggestions are available through apps such as Google Translate, Maps, and Tripadvisor for touring the island on your own.

Cultural Perspectives and Etiquette

Greetings And Gestures
Greeks are known for their welcoming nature and genial temperament. Handshakes, nods, and vocal demonstrations of goodwill are common ways to greet people. When meeting locals, use courteous greetings such as "Yia sas" (hello) or "Kalimera" (good morning). A smile and a respectful demeanor can go a long way toward promoting favorable interactions.

Dining Etiquette
When dining in Corfu, follow local customs and decorum. In restaurants, it is traditional to wait for the host or server to seat you. Greeks enjoy leisurely meals with multiple courses, so avoid rushing through meals. Say "Efharisto" (thank you) to express appreciation for your hospitality and service.

Public Behavior
Respect Corfu's public areas, monuments, and cultural places by following the regulations and guidelines. Dress conservatively when visiting religious locations or attending formal functions. Avoid loud or disruptive behavior in quiet areas, and dispose of trash responsibly to maintain cleanliness and environment.

Festivals and Traditions

Participating in festivals, events, and traditions allows you to experience Corfu's diverse cultural history. Attend religious festivities, such as Easter processions and Saint Spyridon's feast day, to learn about local customs and traditions. Learn about traditional dances, music, and costumes at festivals such as Carnival (Apokries) and Panegyria (religious fairs).

Conclusion

Language and communication play vital roles in enhancing your travel experience in Corfu, Greece. Whether conversing with locals, seeking assistance, or immersing yourself in cultural activities, understanding basic Greek phrases, communication tools, and cultural etiquette can enrich your interactions and create memorable moments on the island. Embrace the linguistic and cultural diversity of Corfu, communicate with kindness and respect, and enjoy the hospitality of this enchanting destination.

Time Zone and Local Customs in Corfu, Greece

Understanding the time zone, local customs, cultural standards, and social etiquette is critical for visitors to Corfu, Greece. In this complete guide, we'll look at time zone variations, traditional customs, social behaviors, and courteous practices to help you have a wonderful and pleasant trip to Corfu.

Time Zone in Corfu

East European Time (EET)

Corfu, like the rest of Greece, uses Eastern European Time (EET), which is UTC+2 during regular time and UTC+3 during daylight saving time. Every year, the switch from standard time to DST takes place in late March (DST begins) and late October (DST ends), influencing Corfu's local time.

During Daylight Savings Time (DST)

Corfu's clocks are set one hour ahead of standard time (UTC+3) during daylight saving time (DST), which lasts from late March until late October. DST attempts to optimize daylight hours in the evenings, resulting in more daylight hours for outdoor activities, sightseeing, and leisure time on Corfu.

Time Zone Conversion

If you're traveling from a different time zone to Corfu, such as Central European Time (CET) or Eastern Standard Time (EST), make sure to change your clocks and calendars accordingly. Determine the local time in Corfu using time zone converters, smartphone apps, or globe clocks, and schedule your activities accordingly.

Local Customs and Cultural Norms

Greetings and Politeness
Greeks place a high priority on politeness, hospitality, and respectful communication in social relationships. When meeting locals or entering establishments, greet people with a smile, nod, or verbal greeting such as "Yia sas" (hello) or "Kalimera" (good morning). Use formal titles (Mr., Mrs., Miss) and last names when addressing elders or strangers.

Punctuality and Timing
While Greeks value punctuality in professional settings and business meetings, social gatherings and informal activities frequently begin later than planned. Allow for flexibility in schedule, particularly during social outings, dinners, and cultural events. Arrive on time for appointments, tours, and reservations to demonstrate respect for others' schedules.

Dining Customs
Dining in Corfu is a social and cultural experience that focuses on hospitality, shared meals, and unhurried dining. Follow these dining etiquettes:

1. Wait for seating: In restaurants, wait for the host or server to assign you a table.
2. Raise your glass for toasts ("Yamas" or "Yia mas") and make eye contact for cheers.

3. Bread and olives: It is usual to begin meals with bread, olives, olive oil, and local appetizers (mezedes).

4. Pace of dining: Greeks enjoy relaxed, multi-course meals with breaks between courses. Don't rush through meals.

5. Payment etiquette: Wait for the host or server to bring the bill (logariasmos) at the end of the meal. Tipping is appreciated but not obligatory.

Social Gestures and Expressions

Greeks use hand gestures, facial expressions, and body language to convey emotions, emphasis, and nonverbal communication. Some common gestures and expressions include:

• Nodding or tilting the head up (ναι) for "yes" and tilting the head down (όχι) for "no."

• Using the open palm gesture (moutza) with fingers spread as a sign of contempt or disagreement (avoid using this gesture).

• Smiling, nodding, and maintaining eye contact during conversations to show engagement and respect.

Dress Code & Attire

When visiting religious sites, formal events, or dining at luxury restaurants, dress modestly and respectfully. Men should dress smart casual (e.g., collared shirts, slacks), while women can wear dresses, skirts, or pants with modest tops.

Beachwear is permissible at beaches and resorts, but please cover up when leaving the beach area.

Public Behavior and Courtesy
Respect Corfu's public areas, monuments, and cultural heritage sites by adhering to the rules, guidelines, and signs. Avoid littering, vandalism, and disruptive behavior in public places. When visiting the city or strolling through congested areas, follow authorized paths, walkways, and pedestrian crossings.

Religious Customs and Observances
Greece has a rich religious tradition, with Orthodox Christianity being the largest religion. When visiting churches, monasteries, or religious sites in Corfu:

1. When entering religious institutions, ladies should dress modestly by covering their shoulders, arms, and knees.
2. Maintain a quiet and respectful manner throughout church prayers and services.
3. Follow guidelines for photography, flash photography, and video recording at religious places.

Cultural Events and Festivals
- **Easter celebrations**

Easter (Pascha) is a significant religious and cultural holiday in Greece, celebrated with somber services, processions, and joyful festivities.

Experience Easter celebrations in Corfu, including the "Pot Throwing" tradition on Holy Saturday, when islanders toss clay pots from balconies to represent new beginnings.

- **Carnival (Apokries)**

In Greece, the Carnival season (Apokries) precedes Lent and is characterized by celebratory parades, masquerades, music, and dance. Celebrate Carnival in Corfu with colorful costumes, street parties, and the traditional "Corfu Carnival" (Karnavali Kerkiras), which includes floats, performances, and cultural events.

- **Saint Spyridon's Feast Day**

Corfu's patron saint, Saint Spyridon, is celebrated for his miracles and protective abilities. Celebrate the feast day of Saint Spyridon on December 12th with religious processions, church services, and cultural events honoring the saint's legacy and significance to the local community.

Local Music and Dance

Immerse yourself in Corfu's musical heritage with traditional music and dance performances. Listen to Corfiot folk songs known as "kantades," which include mandolins, guitars, and emotional lyrics. Local dances like as the "Kalamatianos" and "Sirtaki" can be seen at cultural events and social gatherings.

Customs and Superstitions

Greeks practice a variety of practices, superstitions, and beliefs based on folklore and history.

Some common customs and superstitions in Corfu are:

• Evil eye protection: Use "mati" (eye-shaped charms) or blue beads to ward off the evil eye and bring good luck.

• New Year traditions: Celebrate New Year's Eve with customs like smashing pomegranates for prosperity and cutting a Vasilopita (New Year's cake) to find a hidden coin for luck.

• Name days: Greeks celebrate name days (onomastiki imera) based on saints' feast days, often with gatherings, gifts, and well-wishes for individuals with corresponding names.

Getting to Corfu by Air

Corfu is easily accessible by air, with the island's international airport connecting to major European and global cities. In this article, we'll go over everything you need to know about flying to Corfu, such as airport information, airlines, flight options, airport transfer, and arrival recommendations.

Corfu International Airport(CFU)
Location
Corfu International Airport, also known as Ioannis Kapodistrias Airport (IATA code: CFU), is located on Corfu Island's eastern side, about 3 kilometers south of the island's capital, Corfu Town (Kerkyra).
The airport's strategic location offers easy access to popular tourist resorts, beaches, and attractions across Corfu.

Facilities
Corfu Airport is equipped with modern facilities and services to accommodate passengers' needs:

- **Terminal Buildings:** The airport has a main terminal building for both domestic and international flights, as well as a separate terminal for VIP and private flights.
- **Check-In Counters:** Airlines operating at Corfu Airport have dedicated check-in counters for passengers to complete check-in procedures.
- **Security and Immigration:** Security checks and immigration procedures are conducted efficiently to ensure a smooth departure and arrival experience.
- **Shops and Restaurants:** The airport features duty-free shops, souvenir stores, cafes, and restaurants where passengers can relax and shop before or after their flights.
- **Car Rental Services:** Several car rental companies operate at Corfu Airport, providing convenient options for travelers to rent vehicles for exploring the island.

Airlines and Flight Options

Corfu Airport serves as a gateway to both domestic and international destinations, with airlines offering a range of flight options:

1. International Flights: Airlines such as Aegean Airlines, Ryanair, EasyJet, TUI Airways, Jet2.com, and more operate international flights to Corfu from

various European cities, including London, Berlin, Amsterdam, Rome, Vienna, and Manchester.

2. Domestic Flights: Olympic Air and Sky Express operate domestic flights connecting Corfu with Athens and other Greek islands, providing convenient connections for travelers within Greece.

3. Charter Flights: During the peak tourist season, charter airlines offer direct flights to Corfu from cities across Europe, catering to holidaymakers and package tour travelers.

Flight Duration

The duration of flights to Corfu varies depending on the departure city and airline. Generally, direct flights from major European cities to Corfu have a flight duration of 2 to 4 hours. Connecting flights with layovers may have longer travel times depending on the transit airport and duration of layovers.

Transportation From Corfu Airport

1. Taxi Services: Upon arrival at Corfu Airport, passengers can easily find taxis available outside the terminal building. Licensed taxis operate at fixed rates based on the destination zone within Corfu. Taxis provide a convenient and comfortable option for reaching hotels, resorts, and destinations across the island.

2. Bus Services: Public buses (KTEL) connect Corfu Airport with Corfu Town (Kerkyra) and other major towns and villages on the island. Bus stops are located outside the terminal building, and timetables are available at the airport information desk. Buses offer an affordable transportation option for travelers exploring Corfu's attractions and beaches.

3. Car Rental: For travelers seeking flexibility and independence, car rental services are available at Corfu Airport from reputable companies such as Hertz, Avis, Europcar, and Budget. Renting a car allows travelers to explore Corfu at their own pace, visit remote beaches, and discover hidden gems across the island.

4. Private Transfers: Many hotels, resorts, and tour operators offer private transfer services from the Airport to accommodation properties. Pre-booked private transfers provide personalized service, comfort, and convenience, with professional drivers ensuring a seamless transition from the airport to your destination.

Travel Tips for Arrival

1. Arrive Early: Plan to arrive at Corfu Airport early before your flight's departure time to allow for check-in, security screening, and boarding.
2. Check Flight Status: Stay up to date on your flight's status and any updates or changes to departure or arrival times to avoid any delays or schedule revisions.

3. Pack Essentials: Place your travel documents, passport, tickets, and other necessary goods in your carry-on bag for easy access during check-in and security checks.

4. Currency Exchange: If you need local currency (Euros), exchange money at the airport or use ATMs to withdraw cash upon arrival for immediate expenses.

5. Local Transportation: Familiarize yourself with transportation options from the airport, such as taxis, buses, and car rentals, to reach your accommodation or desired destination.

6. Language: While English is frequently spoken in tourist areas, learning basic Greek phrases will help you communicate with the locals throughout your stay in Corfu.

Conclusion

Traveling to Corfu by plane is a convenient and efficient way to reach this gorgeous island paradise. Arriving at Corfu International Airport, with its contemporary facilities, diverse airline options, and efficient transportation services, is the first step toward a memorable Mediterranean trip. Follow these travel essentials, suggestions, and rules for a seamless and pleasurable arrival, and then set out on a fascinating tour to explore Corfu, Greece's scenic beauties and cultural treasures.

Getting To Corfu By Sea

Corfu, with its azure waters, picturesque coastline, and historical charm, is an enthralling destination accessible by sea. Traveling to Corfu by sea provides a gorgeous and relaxing experience, with numerous ferry routes, cruise options, and port facilities available. In this guide, we'll go over everything you need to know about going to Corfu by sea, such as ferry services, cruise ports, transit alternatives, and arrival recommendations.

1. Ferry Service to Corfu

Domestic ferries

Domestic ferry routes connect Corfu to other Greek islands and mainland ports, making it easy to visit multiple islands and explore the Ionian Sea. Popular ferry routes to Corfu include the following:

1. Igoumenitsa to Corfu: Ferries operate between Igoumenitsa on the Greek mainland and Corfu, offering frequent crossings for passengers and vehicles.
2. Patras to Corfu: Ferries from Patras, a major port in western Greece, provide connections to Corfu for travelers arriving from Athens and other parts of Greece.

3. Bari and Brindisi to Corfu: International ferry routes from Italy, particularly Bari and Brindisi, offer seasonal services to Corfu, linking the island with Italy's Adriatic coast.

International Ferries

During the peak tourist season, international ferry companies operate direct connections to Corfu from neighboring countries and famous tourist locations like as Albania, Montenegro, and Croatia. These international ferry links give travelers more options for visiting Corfu by sea.

Ferry Operators

Corfu is served by several ferry operators, including:

- Ionian Seaways
- Minoan Lines
- Anek Lines
- Superfast Ferries
- Blue Star Ferries
- Ventouris Ferries
- Adriatic Lines
- Red Star Ferries and
- Kerkyra Lines.

Each ferry operator provides varied schedules, vessel types, amenities, and ticket options, allowing travelers to select the best boat service for their needs and travel plans.

2. Cruise Ports in Corfu

Corfu port (Neo Limani)

Corfu Port, also known as Neo Limani (New Port), is the island's primary cruise port, located near Corfu Town (Kerkyra). The port receives a large number of cruise ships and ferries throughout the year, providing docking facilities, passenger services, and connections to the city center and nearby attractions.

Cruise Terminals

Corfu Port features contemporary cruise terminals with facilities for disembarking passengers, customs and immigration, luggage handling, tourist information desks, souvenir stores, and transportation services. Cruise terminals provide a seamless arrival experience for cruise guests visiting Corfu.

Port Facilities

Corfu Port offers a variety of services and amenities to cruise passengers, including:

• Shuttle services: Shuttle buses or taxis are available at the port for transportation to Corfu Town, beaches, and tourist sites.
• Tourist information: Information desks offer maps, brochures, and guidance on sightseeing tours, excursions, and local attractions.

• Shopping and dining: Souvenir shops, cafes, and restaurants are situated near the port for shopping and dining options.

• Transportation options: Car rentals, taxis, and public buses are accessible for exploring Corfu independently or joining organized tours.

Transportation From Corfu Ports

Taxi Services: Taxis are available in Corfu Port (Neo Limani) for easy access to hotels, resorts, beaches, and attractions throughout the island. Licensed taxis operate at predetermined prices based on the destination zone inside Corfu, making them a convenient and efficient option for passengers.

Public Transportation: Corfu Port is served by public buses (KTEL), which link to Corfu Town (Kerkyra), as well as the island's major cities and villages. Bus stops near the port provide economical transportation for travelers visiting Corfu's landmarks, beaches, and cultural institutions.

Car Rentals: Car rental firms have facilities near Corfu Port, where visitors can rent vehicles for self-guided sightseeing of the island. Renting a car offers the flexibility, convenience, and freedom to visit remote areas, scenic viewpoints, and hidden gems in Corfu at your own pace.

Private Transfers: Many hotels, resorts, and tour operators provide private transfers from Corfu Port to lodging sites. Pre-booked private transfers offer personalized attention, comfort, and convenience, with professional drivers that ensure a seamless and enjoyable transfer experience.

Travel Tips For Sea Travel

1. Book Tickets in Advance: To ensure availability and desired travel dates, book ferry and cruise tickets to Corfu in advance, particularly during busy seasons and vacation periods.
2. Check Schedules: Check ferry and cruise schedules, departure hours, and arrival information to plan your trip and make transportation arrangements from the port.
3. Pack Essentials: Keep important goods like travel documents, passports, tickets, and medications in your carry-on bag for convenient access during embarkation and disembarkation.
4. Arrive Early: Arrive at the port early enough before the departure time to complete check-in, security checks, and boarding requirements without rushing.
5. Check Port Facilities: Familiarize yourself with port facilities, services, transportation options, and amenities available at Corfu Port for a comfortable and enjoyable arrival experience.

CHAPTER TWO

Accommodation Options

Hotels And Resorts

1.Ikos Dassia Hotel

Ikos Dassia is a new 5-star resort on Corfu Island, built in a stylish, contemporary Mediterranean style. It is located on the oceanfront at Dassia Beach and has a long sandy beach. Ikos Dassia adheres to the award-winning 'Infinite Lifestyle' concept, ensuring the best levels of quality, service, and entertainment, as well as design and style. The resort has 411 spacious rooms and suites, two main buildings with bedrooms and the resort's main facilities, as well as low-rise bungalow-style rooms, eight restaurants, ten bars, two

Spa centers, indoor and outdoor pools, an open-air theatre, a wide range of sports and watersports facilities, fitness centers, mini clubs, and children's amenities.

Location and Contact Address

Dassia Bay
Dassia, Kerkyra Island, Ionian Islands, Greece 49100
Phone: 00 30 2374 110750 / +30 26614-41600
Fax: +30 237-4099-1510

Languages Spoken
German, Greek, English, French, Italian and Russian

Accepted Payment Methods
Maestro, Mastercard, Visa, Diners Club, American Express, Cash

Check-in   **Check-out**
From 15:00   Until 11:00

Property Facilities

Bathroom	Activities
<ul><li>Toilet paper</li><li>Towels</li><li>Slippers</li><li>Private bathroom</li><li>Toilet</li><li>Free toiletries</li><li>Bathrobe</li><li>Hairdryer</li><li>Shower</li></ul>	<ul><li>Beach</li><li>Evening entertainment</li><li>Kids' club</li><li>Water sport facilities on site</li><li>Entertainment staff</li><li>Diving</li><li>Canoeing</li><li>Windsurfing</li><li>Golf course (within 3 km)</li><li>Tennis court</li></ul>
Bedroom <ul><li>Linen</li><li>Wardrobe or closet</li></ul> **View** <ul><li>Sea View</li></ul>	**Media & Technology** <ul><li>Flat-screen TV</li><li>Cable channels</li><li>Satellite channels</li><li>Telephone</li><li>TV</li></ul>
Outdoors <ul><li>Outdoor furniture</li><li>Beachfront</li><li>Sun terrace</li><li>Terrace</li><li>Garden</li></ul>	**Food & Drink** <ul><li>Fruits</li><li>Wine/champagne</li><li>Kid meals</li><li>Breakfast in the room</li><li>Bar</li><li>Minibar</li><li>Restaurant</li><li>Tea/Coffee maker</li></ul>
Kitchen <ul><li>Electric kettle</li><li>Refrigerator</li></ul> **Room Amenities** <ul><li>Socket near the bed</li></ul> **Living Area** <ul><li>Desk</li></ul>	**Pets** Pets are not allowed.

Reception services	7 swimming pools
• Concierge service • ATM/cash machine on site • Luggage storage • Currency exchange • 24-hour front desk	**Indoor & Outdoor**

Entertainment and family services	Wellness
• Kids' outdoor play equipment • Babysitting/child services	• Personal trainer • Fitness classes

Entertainment and family services
- Kids' outdoor play equipment
- Babysitting/child services

Cleaning services
- Daily housekeeping
- Ironing service
- Dry cleaning
- Laundry

Safety & security
- Safety deposit box

General
- Minimarket on site
- Air conditioning
- Wake-up service
- Tile/marble floor
- Heating
- Soundproofing
- Private entrance
- Car hire
- Lift
- Family rooms
- Barber/beauty shop
- Airport shuttle
- Non-smoking rooms
- Room service

Internet
WiFi is available in all areas and is free of charge.

Parking
Free private parking is possible on site

Wellness
- Personal trainer
- Fitness classes
- Yoga classes
- Full body massage
- Hand massage
- Head massage
- Couples massage
- Foot massage
- Neck massage
- Back massage
- Spa/wellness packages
- Spa lounge/relaxation area
- Steam room
- Spa facilities
- Body scrub
- Body treatments
- Hair styling
- Hair colouring
- Hair cut
- Pedicure
- Manicure
- Facial treatments
- Beauty Services
- Sun umbrellas
- Hot tub/Jacuzzi
- Massage
- Spa and wellness centre
- Fitness centre

The Surroundings of The Facility

Top attractions

Byzantine Museum - 9 km

Mon Repos Palace - 10 km

Butrint National Park - 19 km

What's nearby

Kapodistrias Museum - 5 km

New Fortress - 8 km

Solomos Museum - 9 km

Closest beaches

Dassia Beach - 100 m

Dafnila Beach - 1.1 km

Ipsos Beach - 1.9 km

Eat and Drink

Restaurants

InternationalVenetian Wall - 9 km

Cafes & bars

Leonidas - 500 m

Red Dragon - 600 m

Mouratoros - 1.1 km

Supermarkets & grocery stores

Extra - 350 m

Super Market Dannys - 450 m

Joy Market - 450 m

Transportation
Public transport
Bus StationsBus Station - 9 km
Rail StationsVlor‰ - 92 km

Closest airports
Corfu International Airport - 9 km

2. Grecotel Corfu Imperial

Grecotel Beach Luxe Resort offers lodging with a restaurant, free private parking, a fitness facility, and a garden. It is located in Kommeno, 1.8 km from Dafnila Beach, Corfu Imperial. This five-star resort offers air-conditioned rooms with private bathrooms and a bar. The resort features a 24-hour front desk, a sauna, nighttime entertainment, and an outdoor swimming pool. Every room in the resort has a balcony. In addition to having a kettle, a flat-screen TV, a safety deposit box, and free WiFi, some rooms also have terraces, and some offer views of the sea. Each room has a wardrobe. There's an American breakfast available to guests at Corfu Imperial, Grecotel Beach Luxe Resort. The lodging provides a playground for kids. Darts and table tennis are available. In addition, car and bike rentals are offered. The resort is located 10 km from Port of Corfu and 11 km from New Fortress. The closest airport to Corfu Imperial, Grecotel Beach Luxe Resort is Corfu International Airport, which is located 12 km away.

Location, Address and Contact

Tzavros - Kommeno, Kerkira 490 83, Greece

P.O. Box 130,

GR 49083 Tzavros-Kommeno Corfu, Greece.

Tel: +30 2661 088400 / 00 30 21 1198 8480

Reservations Office

Tel. +30 2661602000

Email: reservations.ci@grecotel.com

Grecotel Corfu Imperial is located on the private Corfu Kommeno peninsula between the towns of Dassia and Gouvia marina near Corfu town.

Languages Spoken

English, French, Russian, German, Greek and Italian

Check-in time: 15:00

Check-out time: 07:00 - 11:00

Accepted Payment Methods

Maestro, Mastercard, Visa, Diners Club, American Express, and Cash.

Property Facilities

Bathroom	Activities
• Toilet paper	• Bicycle rental
• Slippers	• Beach
• Private bathroom	• Tennis equipment
• Toilet	• Evening entertainment
• Free toiletries	• Kids' club
• Bathrobe	• Water sport facilities on site
• Hairdryer	• Entertainment staff
	• Snorkelling
Bedroom	• Diving
• Wardrobe or closet	• Darts
Outdoors	• Table tennis
• Outdoor furniture	• Children's playground
• Beachfront	• Tennis court
• Sun terrace	
• Private beach area	**Food & Drink**
• Balcony	• Special diet menus (on request)
• Terrace	• Breakfast in the room
• Garden	• Bar
	• Minibar
Kitchen	• Restaurant
• Electric kettle	• Tea/Coffee maker
Room Amenities	**Reception services**
• Socket near the bed	• Private check-in/check-out
	• Concierge service
Media & Technology	• Luggage storage
	• Tour desk
• Flat-screen TV	
• Cable channels	• Express check-in/check-out
• Satellite channels	• 24-hour front desk
• Radio	
• Telephone	**Safety & security**
• TV	• Safety deposit box

Internet

WiFi is available in all areas and is free of charge.

Parking

Free private parking is possible on site
- Street parking
- Accessible parking

Entertainment and family services
- Strollers
- Baby safety gates
- Kids' outdoor play equipment
- Indoor play area
- Babysitting/child services

Cleaning services
- Daily housekeeping
- Trouser press
- Ironing service
- Dry cleaning
- Laundry

Business facilities
- Fax/photocopying
- Meeting/banquet facilities

Pets
- Pets are not allowed

Wellness
- Fitness/spa locker rooms
- Personal trainer
- Fitness
- Massage chair
- Spa/wellness packages
- Spa lounge/relaxation area
- Spa facilities
- Body treatments
- Hair styling
- Hair colouring
- Hair cut
- Pedicure
- Manicure
- Hair treatments
- Facial treatments
- Beauty Services
- Sun umbrellas
- Sun loungers or beach chairs
- Massage
- Spa and wellness centre
- Fitness centre
- Sauna

2 swimming pools

Pool 1 - indoorFree!

Pool 2 - outdoorFree!

General
- Shuttle service
- Shared lounge/TV area
- Designated smoking area
- Air conditioning
- Wake-up service
- Soundproofing
- Car hire
- Lift
- Heating
- Family rooms
- Non-smoking rooms
- Room service

The Properties Around The Grecotel Corfu Imperial Hotel. Visitors Cherished Strolling, In The Neighbourhood.

Top Attractions
Byzantine Museum - 6 km
Mon Repos Palace - 8 km
Butrint National Park - 18 km

What's Nearby
Kapodistrias Museum - 4.2 km
New Fortress - 6 km
Solomos Museum - 6 km

Closest Beaches
Dafnila Beach - 1 km
Kontokali Beach - 1.7 km
Gouvia Beach - 1.9 km

Restaurants
InternationalVenetian Wall - 7 km

Cafes & Bars
Pool Bar - 900 m
Toucan beach bar - 1 km
Guapo cocktail bar - 1.4 km

Supermarkets & Grocery Stores
Dafnilas flavours of Corfu - 1.4 km

Super Market Dannys - 1.9 km
Diellas - 2.3 km

Public Transport
Bus StationsBus Station - 7 km
Rail StationsVlor‰ - 94 km

Closest Airports
Corfu International Airport - 7 km

3. MarBella, Mar-Bella Collection

In Agios Ioannis Peristeron, MarBella, Mar-Bella Collection offers free WiFi all over the hotel, a restaurant, a fitness facility, and a sun terrace with a swimming pool. The hotel has a communal lounge and a bar in addition to a garden. The facility features a 24-hour front desk, nighttime entertainment, and a hot tub. The hotel offers a continental, à la carte, or buffet breakfast every morning. The resort has a playground for kids. This five-star resort offers table tennis and tennis, and hiking and cycling are popular activities in the neighborhood. MarBella, Mar-Bella Collection is 400 meters from Agios Ioannis Peristeron Beach, while Tsaki Beach is 1.3 kilometers away from the property. Corfu International Airport is the closest airport, located 19 kilometers away from the lodging, the property offers a paid airport shuttle service.

Address and Contact

Main Street, Agios Ioannis Peristero

490 84, Corfu, Greece

Tel: +30 26610 72400

Email: info@marbella.gr

Check-in	**Check-out**
From 15:00	Until 11:00

No age restriction: There is no age requirement for check-in

Pets
Pets are not allowed.

Languages Spoken
German, Greek, English, French, Italian, Portuguese, Russian, and Slovenian

Accepted Payment Methods
Mastercard, Visa, Diners Club, American Express, and Cash

Property Facilities

Outdoors	Activities
Outdoor furniture Beachfront Sun terrace Terrace Garden	Bicycle rental Aerobics Live sport events (broadcast) Live music/performance Themed dinner nights Walking tours
Food & Drink	Movie nights
Fruits Wine/champagne Kid-friendly buffet Kid meals Special diet menus (on request) Snack bar Breakfast in the room Bar (Temporarily closed) Restaurant (Temporarily closed)	Beach Tennis equipment Water park Evening entertainment Kids' club Water sport facilities on site Entertainment staff Snorkelling Cycling Hiking
Internet WiFi is available in all areas and is free of charge.	Canoeing Karaoke Table tennis
Parking No parking available.	Children's playground Games room Tennis court
Reception services	**Entertainment and family services**
Invoice provided Concierge service ATM/cash machine on site Luggage storage Tour desk Currency exchange 24-hour front desk	Strollers Baby safety gates Kids' outdoor play equipment Indoor play area Board games/puzzles Babysitting/child services

Cleaning services Daily housekeeping Ironing service Dry cleaning Laundry	**Business facilities** Fax/photocopying Business centre Meeting/banquet facilities
Safety & security Fire extinguishers Smoke alarms Security alarm Key card access 24-hour security Safety deposit box	**General** Minimarket on site Shared lounge/TV area Designated smoking area Air conditioning Non-smoking throughout Heating Car hire Packed lunches
3 outdoor swimming pools Infinity pool Salt-water pool Pool/beach towels Sun loungers or beach chairs Sun umbrellas Pool bar All ages welcome	Chapel/shrine Soundproof rooms Lift Family rooms Airport shuttle Non-smoking rooms Room service
Wellness Neck massage Back massage Spa/wellness packages Spa lounge/relaxation area Steam room Light therapy Body wrap / scrub Body treatments Hair styling, cut & colouring Hammam Hot tub/Jacuzzi	Personal trainer Yoga classes Fitness Full body massage Hand massage Head massage Couples massage Foot massage Pedicure & Manicure Make up services Facial treatments

Property Surroundings
Great location guests loved walking around.

Top Attractionsn Around The Facility
- Serbian Museum - 12 km
- Asian Art Museum - 13 km
- Byzantine Museum - 13 km

What's Nearby
- Achilleion Palace - 6 km
- Mon Repos Palace - 11 km
- Trion Martiron Park - 11 km

Closest Beaches
- Agios Ioannis Peristeron Beach - 150 m
- Tsaki Beach - 1.2 km
- Moraitika Beach - 2.3 km

Restaurants
- InternationalVenetian Wall - 13 km

Cafes & Bars
- Kahlua Greek Bar- 50 m
- Buddies - 2.6 km
- Enjoy - 2.6 km

Supermarkets & Grocery Stores
- Coop - 2.4 km
- 3K's - 3.2 km

- Joras - 3.3 km

Transportation Options
Public transport
- Bus StationsBus Station - 11 km

Closest Airports
- Corfu International Airport - 9 km

4. Domes Miramare, A Luxury Collection Resort

Domes Miramare, A Luxury Collection Resort, is well-known for its luxurious accommodations with views of the ocean and a serene beachfront setting that oozes elegance. On the other hand, a few visitors have voiced complaints regarding the housekeeping's promptness and cleanliness. Although the hotel's location near the beach is typically commended for its picturesque qualities, some people may find the neighboring road to be noisy. While the facilities, which include many pools and excellent cuisine, are well-received, some travelers feel that the services are too expensive for what they get. Guest pleasure appears to be impacted by variations in service quality.

Address and Contact

Miramare Beach, Moraitika Corfu 49100 Greece

Phone: +30 2661 440500 / 00 1 844-631-0595

Reservation: (+30) 2310 840 550

Email: concierge@domesmiramare.com

Check-in	Check-out
15:00 - 00:00	10:30 - 11:00

Accepted Payment Methods

Mastercard, Visa, Discover, JCB, Diners Club, American Express, and Cash

Hotel Style

- Luxury and Trendy

Property Facilities

Bathroom	Activities
• Towels	• Live music/performance
• Slippers	• Tour or class about local culture
• Private bathroom	• Bike tours
• Toilet	• Walking tours
• Free toiletries	• Temporary art galleries
• Bathrobe	• Beach
• Hairdryer	• Evening entertainment
• Shower	• Water sport facilities on site
	• Horse riding
Bedroom	• Cycling
• Linen	• Hiking
• Wardrobe or closet	• Tennis court
• Alarm clock	
	Food & Drink
Outdoors	• Coffee house on site
• Outdoor furniture	• Fruits
• Beachfront	• Wine/champagne
• Sun terrace	• Special diet menus (on request)
• Private beach area	• Snack bar
• Terrace	• Breakfast in the room
• Garden	• Bar
Kitchen	• Minibar
• Coffee machine	• Restaurant
Room Amenities	
• Socket near the bed	**Reception Services**
Pets	• Private check-in/check-out
Pets are allowed on request.	• Concierge service
	• Luggage storage
Media & Technology	• Currency exchange
• Flat-screen TV	• Express check-in/check-out
• Radio	• 24-hour front desk
• Telephone	

Internet	General
WiFi is available in all areas and is free of charge.	• Adult only • Shared lounge/TV area
Parking	• Designated smoking area
Free private parking is possible on site • Electric vehicle charging station	• Air conditioning • Allergy-free room • Wake-up service
Cleaning services	• Heating
• Daily housekeeping • Trouser press • Ironing service • Dry cleaning	• Car hire • Packed lunches • Lift • Ironing facilities • Facilities for disabled guests
Business facilities	• Non-smoking rooms
• Fax/photocopying	• Iron • Room service

Wellness	
• Yoga classes	• Body wrap & scrub
• Full body massage	• Body treatments
• Hand massage	• Hair styling
• Head massage	• Hair cut
• Couples massage	• Pedicure & Manicure
• Foot massage	• Hair treatments
• Neck massage	• Make up services
• Back massage	• Facial treatments
• Spa/wellness packages	• Beauty Services
• Steam room	• Hammam
• Light therapy	• Spa lounge/relaxation area

Accessibility	Safety & Security
• Visual aids: Braille • Emergency cord in bathroom • Lower bathroom sink • Higher level toilet • Toilet with grab rails • Wheelchair accessible	• Fire extinguishers • CCTV outside property • Smoke alarms • Security alarm • Key card access • 24-hour security • Safety deposit box
3 Outdoor Swimming Pools	
• Open all year • Pool with view • Shallow end	• Pool/beach towels • Pool bar • Sun loungers or beach chairs

Property Surroundings

Top Attractions

- Serbian Museum - 14 km
- Asian Art Museum - 15 km
- Byzantine Museum - 15 km

What's Nearby

- Achilleion Palace - 8 km
- Mon Repos Palace - 12 km
- Trion Martiron Park - 13 km

Closest Beaches

- Moraitika Beach - 350 m
- Messonghi Beach - 1.1 km
- Agios Ioannis Peristeron Beach - 1.5 km

Restaurants

- InternationalVenetian Wall - 15 km

Cafes & Bars

- Buddies - 750 m
- Enjoy - 750 m
- Caldera Bar - 800 m

Supermarkets & Grocery Stores

- Coop - 600 m
- 3K's - 1.3 km
- Joras - 1.4 km

Transportation Options

Public Transport

- Bus StationsBus Station - 13 km

Closest Airports

- Corfu International Airport - 11 km

5. Corfu Pelagos Hotel

The Corfu Pelagos Hotel offers lodging with a restaurant, free private parking, a fitness centre, and a garden, and is located in Moraitika, 500 metres from Moraitika Beach. This 4-star hotel offers complimentary WiFi, a bar, and a terrace. Room service and nightly entertainment are offered by the lodging.

Air-conditioned rooms with desks, kettles, safety deposit boxes, TVs, balconies, and private bathrooms with bathtubs will be available to hotel guests. The Corfu Pelagos Hotel offers accommodations with seating areas in the rooms. Continental, full English/Irish, and buffet breakfasts are available every day. In addition to having a car and bike rental option, the lodging offers table tennis.

The Corfu Pelagos Hotel is located 1.7 kilometres from Messonghi Beach and 2.1 km from Agios Ioannis Peristeron Beach. The hotel is located 22 kilometres from Corfu International Airport, and it provides a payable airport shuttle service.

Contact Address

Moraitika 49084 Greece, Corfu

Tel: +30 26610 77060/ +30 694 026 6608
Email: info@corfupelagos.com

Accepted Payment Methods

Maestro, Mastercard, Visa, UnionPay credit card, and Cash.

Check-In	**Check-Out**
13:30 - 23:30	Until 11:00

Property Facilities

Bathroom	Activities
• Toilet paper • Towels • Private bathroom • Toilet • Free toiletries • Hairdryer • Bath	• Bicycle rental • Bingo • Live music/performance • Tour or class about local culture • Happy hour • Bike tours • Walking tours • Beach
Bedroom • Wardrobe or closet	• Evening entertainment • Horse riding
View • Mountain view • Garden view • Ocean View	• Diving • Cycling • Hiking • Table tennis
Outdoors • Outdoor fireplace • Outdoor furniture • Sun terrace • Balcony • Terrace • Garden	**Living Area** • Sofa • Fireplace • Seating Area • Desk
Kitchen • Electric kettle • Kitchenette	**Food & Drink** • Coffee house on site • Special diet menus (on request) • Snack bar • Breakfast in the room
Room Amenities • Sofa bed • Drying rack for clothing • Clothes rack	• Bar • Restaurant
Media & Technology • TV	**Internet** WiFi is available in public areas and is free of charge.

Parking Free private parking is available on site	**Wellness** • Fitness • Sun umbrellas
Reception Services • Invoice provided • Private check-in/check-out • Luggage storage • Express check-in/check-out	• Sun loungers or beach chairs • Fitness centre • Spa Facilities
	Business facilities • Fax/photocopying
Cleaning Services • Daily housekeeping • Ironing service • Dry cleaning • Laundry	**Safety & security** • Fire extinguishers • CCTV in common areas • Smoke alarms • Security alarm • Key access
General • Shuttle service • Air conditioning • Tile/marble floor • Soundproofing • Private entrance • Car hire • Soundproof rooms • Family rooms • Airport shuttle • Non-smoking rooms • Room service	• 24-hour security • Safety deposit box **Accessibility** • Upper floors accessible by stairs only Outdoor swimming pool

Property surroundings
Restaurants
- InternationalVenetian Wall - 15 km

Cafes & Bars
- Buddies - 250 m
- Enjoy - 300 m

- Planet Café - 350 m

Supermarkets & Grocery Stores
- Coop - 100 m
- 3K's - 850 m
- Joras – 950 m

Top Attractions
- Serbian Museum - 15 km
- Asian Art Museum - 15 km
- Byzantine Museum - 15 km

What's Nearby
- Achilleion Palace - 8 km
- Mon Repos Palace - 13 km
- Trion Martiron Park - 13 km

Closest Beaches
- Moraitika Beach - 350 m
- Messonghi Beach - 800 m
- Agios Ioannis Peristeron Beach - 1.9 km

Transportation Options
Public transport
- Bus StationsBus Station - 14 km

Closest airports
- Corfu International Airport - 11 km

6. Acanthus Blue

In Corfu Town, Acanthus Blue comes with a restaurant, bar, garden, and terrace. The Serbian Museum, Ionio University, and Municipal Gallery are just a short distance away from this site. The lodging offers room service, tours, and a front desk staffed around the clock. Every room at the hotel has a desk in it. Coffee makers, flat-screen TVs, safety deposit boxes, free WiFi, and balconies or sea views are standard amenities in all of the hotel's rooms. Every accommodation has a private bathroom, bed linens, and bathrobes. There are three alternatives for breakfast each day: à la carte, Full English/Irish, and vegetarian. Bicycle rentals are offered at Acanthus Blue. The area is a popular riding destination. Panagia Vlahernon Church, Mon Repos Palace, and Royal Baths Mon Repos are a few of the well-known attractions close to the lodging. Corfu International Airport, located one kilometer away from Acanthus Blue, is the closest airport.

Contact Address
8-12 3rd parodos Mitropolitou Athanasiou street Kerkira 491 00, Corfu Town. Greece
Tel: +302661044059

Accepted Payment Methods

Maestro, Mastercard, Visa, Diners Club, American Express, Cash

Hotel Style
✓ Romantic
✓ Quaint

Languages Spoken
English, Afrikaans, and Greek

Check-in
14:00 - 00:00
Check-out
05:00 - 11:00

No age restriction. There is no age requirement for check-in

Pets

• Pets are not allowed.

Property Facilities

Bathroom	Internet
	WiFi is available in all areas and is free of charge.
• Towels	
• Slippers	
• Private bathroom	**Parking**
	Free public parking is availablee at a location nearby
• Free toiletries	
• Bathrobe	• Street parking
• Hairdryer	
• Shower	**Reception services**
	• Private check-in/check-out
Bedroom	• Concierge service
• Linen	• Luggage storage
• Wardrobe or closet	• Tour desk
	• Express check-in/check-out
Outdoors	• 24-hour front desk
• Outdoor furniture	
• Sun terrace	**Cleaning services**
• Terrace	• Daily housekeeping
• Garden	• Trouser press
	• Ironing service
Kitchen	• Laundry
• Coffee machine	
• Electric kettle	**Safety & security**
	• Fire extinguishers
Room Amenities	• Smoke alarms
• Clothes rack	• Key card access
	• 24-hour security
Activities	• Safety deposit box
• Bicycle rental	
• Cycling	**Food & Drink**
	• Coffee house on site
Living Area	• Wine/champagne
• Desk	• Special diet menus (on request)
	• Snack bar
Media & Technology	• Breakfast in the room
• Streaming service (like Netflix)	
• Flat-screen TV	• Bar
• Telephone	• Minibar
• TV	• Restaurant
	• Tea/Coffee maker

General	Wellness
<ul><li>Shuttle service</li><li>Designated smoking area</li><li>Air conditioning</li><li>Non-smoking throughout</li><li>Wake-up service</li><li>Hardwood or parquet floors</li><li>Heating</li><li>Soundproofing</li><li>Laptop safe</li><li>Soundproof rooms</li><li>Facilities for disabled guests</li><li>Pants press</li><li>Non-smoking rooms</li><li>Room service</li></ul>	<ul><li>Massage</li><li>Kids' pool</li><li>Personal trainer</li><li>Fitness</li><li>Hair styling</li><li>Hair cut</li><li>Spa and wellness centre</li><li>Fitness centre</li><li>Beauty Services</li><li>Spa/wellness packages</li></ul>
	Accessibility
	<ul><li>Wheelchair accessible</li></ul>

Property Surroundings

Top Attractions
- Asian Art Museu - 1.7 km
- Byzantine Museum - 1.8 km
- Butrint National Park - 19 km

What's Nearby
- Trion Martiron Park - 50 m
- Ntougkla Square - 400 m
- Mon Repos Palace - 550 m

Closest Beach
- Royal Baths Mon Repos - 400 m

Restaurants
- International Venetian Wall - 1.7 km

Cafes & Bars
- Pool Bar - 400 m
- Royal Baths Mon Repos - 400 m
- Kaphes me Zaxarè - 400 m

Supermarkets & Grocery Stores
- Sconto Market - 10 m
- Super Deal Market - 50 m

- Family Supermarket - 1.1 km

Public Transport

- Bus StationsBus Station - 950 m

Closest airports

- Corfu International Airport -1 km

7. Angsana Corfu Resort & Spa
The first Banyan Tree Hotels & Resorts location in Europe, Angsana Corfu Resort & Spa, exemplifies a distinctive approach to hospitality with its tasteful 196 rooms, suites, and Mediterranean villas with private pools, all blending traditional Greek hospitality with Asian influences.

Angsana Corfu is the best place to discover the island's natural beauty because it's only 12 km south of the airport and Corfu Town, a UNESCO World Heritage site. In addition to offering an unparalleled view of Benitses Bay and the surrounding coastline, this breathtaking position is close to historic places, must-see sights, and spectacular sandy beaches. Activities catering to all interests can also be found nearby. Angsana Corfu is a luxury and picturesque getaway where every corner offers a different experience. It is perched high on a lush slope overlooking the Ionian Sea.

Contact Address

11th Km National Road Akra Punta, Benitses 49084 Greece

Tel: 00 30 2661 022900

Email: reservations-corfu@angsana.com

Check-in   **Check-out**
15:00 - 00:00   **04:00 - 11:00**

Age restriction: The minimum age for check-in is 18

Pets

- Pets are allowed. Charges may be applicable.

Accepted Payment Methods

Maestro, Mastercard, Visa, Diners Club, and Cash

Languages Spoken

English, Russian, Greek, Italian, German, and French

Property Facilities

Bathroom
- Toilet paper
- Towels
- Bath or shower
- Slippers
- Private bathroom
- Toilet
- Free toiletries
- Bathrobe
- Hairdryer

Bedroom
- Linen
- Wardrobe or closet

Outdoors
- Outdoor furniture
- Sun terrace
- Private beach area
- Terrace
- Garden

Kitchen
- Coffee machine
- Electric kettle

Room Amenities
- Socket near the bed
- Clothes rack

Media & Technology
- Flat-screen TV
- Radio

Internet
WiFi is available in all areas and is free of charge.

Activities
- Bicycle rental
- Aerobics
- Live music/performance
- Cooking class
- Tour or class about local culture
- Themed dinner nights
- Bike tours
- Walking tours
- Beach
- Kids' club
- Water sport facilities on site
- Entertainment staff
- Snorkelling
- Horse riding
- Diving
- Hiking
- Canoeing

Living Area
- Sofa
- Seating Area
- Desk

Food & Drink
- Coffee house on site
- Fruits
- Wine/champagne
- Kid meals
- Special diet menus (on request)
- Snack bar
- Breakfast in the room
- Bar (Temporarily closed)
- Minibar
- Restaurant
- Tea/Coffee maker

Parking

Free private parking is available
- Valet parking
- Parking garage
- Accessible parking

Reception Services
- Invoice provided
- Lockers
- Private check-in/check-out
- Concierge service
- Luggage storage
- Express check-in/check-out
- 24-hour front desk

Entertainment and family services
- Indoor play area
- Board games/puzzles
- Babysitting/child services

Cleaning Services
- Daily housekeeping
- Trouser press
- Ironing service
- Dry cleaning
- Laundry

Accessibility
- Emergency cord in bathroom
- Lower bathroom sink
- Toilet with grab rails
- Wheelchair accessible

Business Facilities
- Meeting/banquet facilities

Safety & security
- Fire extinguishers
- CCTV outside property
- CCTV in common areas
- Smoke alarms
- Security alarm
- Key card access
- 24-hour security
- Safety deposit box

General
- Shared lounge/TV area
- Air conditioning
- Non-smoking throughout
- Tile/marble floor
- Heating
- Soundproofing
- Car hire
- Laptop safe
- Packed lunches
- Soundproof rooms
- Lift
- Family rooms
- Barber/beauty shop
- Facilities for disabled guests
- Non-smoking rooms
- Room service

3 swimming pools - Indoor and outdoor(kids &Adult)	Wellness
• All ages welcome	• Fitness classes
• Infinity pool	• Yoga classes
• Pool with view	• Massage chair
• Pool/beach towels	• Full body massage
• Pool bar	• Spa/wellness packages
• Sun loungers or beach chairs	• Spa lounge/relaxation area
• Sun umbrellas	• Steam room
• Heated pool	• Spa facilities
• Shallow end	• Hair styling
	• Hair cut
	• Beauty Services
	• Hot tub/Jacuzzi

Property Surroundings

Top Attractions
- Serbian Museum - 7 km
- Asian Art Museum - 8 km
- Byzantine Museum - 8 km

What's Nearby
- Achilleion Palace - 1 km
- Mon Repos Palace - 6 km
- Trion Martiron Park - 6 km

Closest Beaches

- Kaiser Bridge Beach - 900 m
- Benitses Beach - 1.2 km
- Aeolos Beach - 1.4 km

Restaurants
- International Venetian Wall - 8 km

Cafes & Bars
- Kostas's Bar Walkers Point - 2.3 km
- Monte Café - 2.6 km
- Beach Bar - 2.9 km

Supermarkets & Grocery Stores
- Coop - 950 m
- Alexandros Supermarket - 1.6 km

Public Transport
- Bus Stations - 6 km

Closest Airports
- Corfu International Airport - 4.2 km

8. The Olivar Suites

The Olivar Suites offers lodging with a restaurant, free private parking, a seasonal outdoor pool, and a fitness facility. It is situated in Mesongi, 200 meters from Messonghi Beach. The five-star hotel offers air-conditioned rooms with private bathrooms and a courtyard. The lodging provides visitors with a front desk manned around the clock, room service, and currency exchange. Every room in the hotel has a wardrobe. Each accommodation features a kettle, a flat-screen TV, free WiFi, a safety deposit box, and in some cases, a terrace with views of the sea. Every room at The Olivar Suites has towels and bed linens. The hotel offers a continental, buffet, or vegan breakfast.

In addition, the lodging has a wellness center with a sauna and other services for visitors to enjoy. The Olivar Suites offers both vehicle and bike rentals in an area that is well-known for cycling. The hotel is located 1.8 km from Moraitika Beach and 12 km from Achilleion Palace. The Olivar Suites is 24 kilometers from Corfu International Airport, the closest airport.

Contact Information

Address: Messonghi, 490 80 Corfu, Greece

Phone: +302661080300

Email: sales@olivarsuites.gr

Websites: https://www.olivarsuites.gr/

Languages Spoken

- German
- Greek
- English
- French

Property Facilities

Bathroom	Activities
Toilet paper	Bicycle rental
Towels	Live music/performance
Slippers	Cooking class
Private bathroom	Themed dinner nights
Toilet	Bike tours
Free toiletries	Walking tours
Bathrobe	Beach
Hairdryer	Water sport facilities on site
	Cycling & Hiking

Bedroom	Cleaning services
Linen	Daily housekeeping
Wardrobe or closet	Ironing service
	Laundry & Dry cleaning
Outdoors	**Media & Technology**
Picnic area	Flat-screen TV
Outdoor furniture	Cable channels
Beachfront	Telephone
Sun terrace	**Internet**
Private beach area	WiFi is available in all areas and is free of charge.
Terrace	
Garden	**Parking**
	Free private parking
	Street parking
Kitchen	Valet parking
Electric kettle	Electric vehicle charging station
Room Amenities	Accessible parking
Drying rack for clothing	
Pets	**Reception services**
Pets are allowed on request. Charges may be applicable.	Invoice provided
	Private check-in/check-out
Food & Drink	Concierge service
Fruits	Luggage storage
Wine/champagne	Currency exchange
Kid-friendly buffet	24-hour front desk
Special diet menus (on request)	
Snack bar	**Entertainment and family services**
Breakfast in the room	Babysitting/child services
Bar/ Restaurant	
Tea/Coffee maker	

Safety & security	Wellness
Fire extinguishers	Personal trainer
CCTV outside property	Fitness classes
Smoke alarms	Yoga classes
Key card access	Full body massage
24-hour security	Spa/wellness packages
Safety deposit box	Spa lounge/relaxation area
General	Pedicure & Manicure
Shuttle service	Beauty Services
Air conditioning	Spa and wellness centre
Non-smoking throughout	Sauna
Wake-up service	**Accessibility**
Heating	Lower bathroom sink
Soundproofing	Higher level toilet
Private entrance	Toilet with grab rails
Car hire	Wheelchair accessible
Fan	**Outdoor swimming pool**
Family rooms	All ages welcome
Facilities for disabled guests	Pool with view
Non-smoking rooms	Pool/beach towels
Iron	Pool bar
Room service	Sun loungers or beach chairs
	Sun umbrellas

Property Surroundings The Olivar Suites

Top Attractions
- Serbian Museum - 16 km
- Asian Art Museum - 16 km
- Byzantine Museum - 16 km

What's Nearby
- Achilleion Palace - 9 km
- Mon Repos Palace - 14 km
- Trion Martiron Park - 15 km

Closest Beaches

- Messonghi Beach - 10 m
- Moraitika Beach

Restaurants
- InternationalVenetian Wall - 16 km

Cafes & Bars
- Barocco Messogi - 150 m
- Oasis - 200 m
- Palla - 450 m

Supermarkets & Grocery Stores
- General Market - 50 m
- 3K's - 100 m
- Joras - 600 m

Public Transport
Bus Station - 15 km

Closest Airports
Corfu International Airport - 12 km

9. Hotel Rossis

Hotel Rossis, a five-star hotel in Mesongi with a restaurant, garden, and bar, is fronting the beach. The property is located 12 miles from Achilleion Palace, 1.7 km from Moraitika Beach, and only a few steps from Messonghi Beach. The lodging provides visitors with luggage storage, a communal lounge, and a front desk manned around the clock. Every room at the hotel has a desk. Each accommodation features a kettle, a flat-screen TV, free WiFi, a safety deposit box, and in some cases, a terrace with views of the sea. Each unit has a private bathroom, bed linens, and a hair dryer. Skiing and cycling are popular in the area, and Hotel Rossis has automobile rentals. 14 kilometers separate Pontikonisi from the accommodation, while New Fortress is 22 km away. The nearest airport is Corfu International, 24 km from Hotel Rossis, and the property offers a paid airport shuttle service.

Contact Information

Address: Messonghi

Postal code (ZIP): 49080

City/Location: Corfu

Phone: +302661075352

https://rossisbeachhotel.com/

Check-in policy
Check-in time: 15:00

Check-out time: 11:00

Languages Spoken

Greek, English

Property Facilities

Bathroom	Living Area
Toilet paper	Desk
Towels	
Private bathroom	**Media & Technology**
Toilet	Flat-screen TV
Free toiletries	Satellite channels
Hairdryer	Telephone
Shower	TV
Bedroom	**Food & Drink**
Linen	Coffee house on site
Wardrobe or closet	Fruits
	Wine/champagne
Outdoors	Kid meals
Outdoor furniture	Snack bar
Beachfront	Bar
Sun terrace	Restaurant
Terrace	
Garden	**Internet**
	WiFi is available in all areas and is free of charge.
Kitchen	
Electric kettle	**Parking**
Refrigerator	No parking available.
Cleaning services	**Reception services**
Daily housekeeping	Lockers
Business facilities	Luggage storage
Fax/photocopying	24-hour front desk

General	Wellness
Shuttle service	Sun umbrellas
Shared lounge/TV area	Sun loungers or beach chairs
Air conditioning	Fitness
Non-smoking throughout	Spa Services
Wake-up service	Massage
Tile/marble floor	
Heating	**Safety & security**
Soundproofing	Fire extinguishers
Car hire	Smoke alarms
Family rooms	Security alarm
Airport shuttle	24-hour security
Non-smoking rooms	Safety deposit box

Activities	
Bike tours	Windsurfing
Walking tours	Billiards
Beach	Games room
Snorkelling	Skiing
Diving	Fishing
Cycling	Canoeing
Hiking	

The Environs Of The Property

Top Attractions
- Serbian Museum - 16 km
- Asian Art Museum - 16 km
- Byzantine Museum - 16 km

What's Nearby
- Achilleion Palace – 12 m
- Mon Repos Palace - 14 km
- Trion Martiron Park - 14 km

Closest Beaches
- Messonghi Beach - 0 m
- Moraitika Beach - 400 m
- Agios Ioannis Peristeron Beach - 3 km

Restaurants
- International Venetian Wall -16 km

Cafes & Bars
- Barocco Messogi - 50 m
- Oasis - 100 m
- Zefyros Beach Bar - 300 m

Supermarkets & Grocery Stores
- General Market - 300 m
- 3K's - 350 m
- Joras - 550 m

Public Transport
Bus Station - 15 km

Closest airports
Corfu International Airport - 12 km

10. Rodostamo Hotel & Spa- Adults Friendly

Hotel Rossis, a five-star hotel in Mesongi with a restaurant, garden, and bar, is fronting the beach. The property is located 12 miles from Achilleion Palace, 1.7 km from Moraitika Beach, and only a few steps from Messonghi Beach. The lodging provides visitors with luggage storage, a communal lounge, and a front desk manned around the clock. Every room at the hotel has a desk. Each accommodation features a kettle, a flat-screen TV, free WiFi, a safety deposit box, and in some cases, a terrace with views of the sea. Each unit has a private bathroom, bed linens, and a hair dryer. Skiing and cycling are popular in the area, and Hotel Rossis has automobile rentals. 14 kilometers separate from Pontikonisi from the accommodation, while New Fortress is 22 km away. The nearest airport is Corfu International, 24 km from Hotel Rossis, and the property offers a paid airport shuttle service.

Contact Address

Rodostamo Hotel & Spa

Kommeno, Corfu 49100, Greece

Tel. +30 26614 40300

Email: info@rodostamo.gr

Website: rodostamo.gr

Languages Spoken

- German
- Greek
- English
- French
- Italian
- Albanian

Check-in   **Check-out**

14:00 - 00:00   **07:00 - 11:00**

Age restriction: The minimum age for check-in is 18

Pets

- Pets are not allowed.

Accepted Payment Methods

Maestro, Mastercard, Visa, American Express, and Cash

Property Facilities

Bathroom	Activities
• Toilet paper	• Bicycle rental
• Towels	• Live sport events (broadcast)
• Bidet	• Live music/performance
• Slippers	• Bike tours
• Private bathroom	• Evening entertainment
• Toilet	• Water sport facilities on site
• Free toiletries	• Snorkelling
• Hairdryer	• Horse riding
• Shower	• Diving
	• Cycling
Bedroom	• Canoeing
• Linen	• Skiing
• Wardrobe or closet	• Fishing
Outdoors	**Living Area**
• Outdoor furniture	• Desk
• Sun terrace	
• Terrace	**Media & Technology**
• Garden	• Flat-screen TV
	• Cable channels
Kitchen	• Satellite channels
• Electric kettle	• Radio
	• Telephone
Room Amenities	• TV
• Socket near the bed	
• Drying rack for clothing	**Food & Drink**
• Clothes rack	• Coffee house on site
	• Fruits
Ski	• Wine/champagne
	• Special diet menus (on request)
• Ski school	• Snack bar
	• Breakfast in the room
Internet	• Bar (Temporarily closed)
WiFi is available in all areas and is free of charge.	• Restaurant (Temporarily closed)

Parking	General
Free private parking is available on site	
• Valet parking	• Shuttle service
• Electric vehicle charging station	• Grocery deliveries
• Accessible parking	• Minimarket on site
	• Shared lounge/TV area
	• Air conditioning
Reception Services	• Non-smoking throughout
• Invoice provided	• Wake-up service
• Lockers	• Tile/marble floor
• Concierge service	• Heating
• ATM/cash machine on site	• Car hire
• Luggage storage	• Laptop safe
• Tour desk	• Packed lunches
• 24-hour front desk	• Soundproof rooms
	• Lift
Entertainment and Family Services	• Family rooms
• Board games/puzzles	• Ironing facilities
	• Facilities for disabled guests
Cleaning Services	• Airport shuttle
• Daily housekeeping	• Non-smoking rooms
• Trouser press	• Iron
• Ironing service	• Wake up service/Alarm clock
• Dry cleaning	• Room service
• Laundry	
	Safety & Security
Business Facilities	• Fire extinguishers
• Fax/photocopying	• CCTV in common areas
• Business centre	• Smoke alarms
• Meeting/banquet facilities	• Security alarm
	• Key card access
	• 24-hour security
	• Safety deposit box

Wellness	
• Fitness • Massage chair • Spa/wellness packages • Foot bath • Spa lounge/relaxation area • Steam room • Spa facilities • Body scrub • Hair styling • Hair cut • Pedicure & Manicure	• Waxing services • Beauty Services • Sun umbrellas • Sun loungers or beach chairs • Hammam • Hot tub/Jacuzzi • Massage • Spa and wellness centre • Sauna • Hair treatments • Make up services
Accessibility	**2 Outdoor Swimming Pools**
• Lower bathroom sink • Toilet with grab rails • Wheelchair accessible • Entire unit wheelchair accessible	• Pool with view • Pool/beach towels • Pool bar • Sun loungers or beach chairs • Heated pool • Plunge pool

The surroundings of the property

Top Attractions
- Byzantine Museum - 7 km
- Mon Repos Palace - 9 km
- Butrint National Park - 19 km

What's Nearby
- Kapodistrias Museum - 4.1 km
- New Fortress - 7 km
- Solomos Museum - 7 km

Closest Beaches
- Dafnila Beach - 800 m
- Gouvia Beach - 1.1 km
- Dassia Beach - 1.4 km

Restaurants
- International Venetian Wall - 7 km

Cafes & Bars
- Guapo cocktail bar - 150 m
- CAFé Mé - 300 m
- Pool Bar - 300 m

Supermarkets & Grocery Stores
- Dafnilas - Flavours of Corfu - 350 m
- Super Market Danny - 1.2 km
- Diellas - 1.4 km

Public Transport
- Bus Station - 7 km
- Rail Station Vlor‰ - 94 km

Closest Airports
- Corfu International Airpor - 7 km

Boutique Hotels in Corfu

1. Corfu Mare Hotel

The Corfu Mare Hotel is an adults-only boutique hotel in Corfu Town's serene area. It is surrounded by lush nature and is around 650 meters from the port, 3 kilometers from the airport, and 1.5 kilometers from Corfu Town. The hotel is renowned for its Venetian architecture, relaxing setting, and traditional Corfiot hospitality.

Guests can take advantage of a variety of services, including a massage service, swimming pool, conference center, restaurant and bar, and gym. The hotel also offers a variety of room types, from regular rooms to premium suites, all fitted with modern conveniences and intended for comfort, including CocoMat beds and pillows.

For visitors looking to explore the local area, there are various restaurants and attractions nearby, including Indian and Mediterranean cuisine, seafood, cafes, and mystery locations like the Fortress Of Secrets - Escape Rooms Corfu, Greece.

It is an excellent alternative for those looking for a calm escape with convenient access to Corfu Town's colorful activities. If you're planning a vacation, it's preferable to book directly with the hotel to get the lowest pricing and additional services like flexible cancellation and airport transfers.

Corfu is well-known for its lovely beaches, and the Corfu Mare Hotel is located near several of the best. Here are a few choices:

- **Mon Repos Beach:** A beautiful beach about 3 kilometers from the hotel that offers a tranquil atmosphere and clear waters.

- **Garitsa Bay:** Although not a classic sandy beach, Garitsa Bay provides a lengthy stretch of coastline with views of the Old Fortress, located about 2 kilometers from the hotel.

- **Alykes Potamou:** Located around 5 kilometers north of Corfu Town, this beach is recognized for its shallow waters and family-friendly atmosphere.

- For those willing to travel a little further, the west coast of Corfu has a couple of the island's most famous beaches, such as Glyfada and Agios Gordios, which are around 15-20 kilometers away but worth the trip for their expansive sandy shores and scenic beauty.

Transportation Options
Guests staying at the Corfu Mare Hotel may explore the beautiful island of Corfu using an array of local transportation options:

Bus: KTEL Kerkyras operates a local bus service that connects the Corfu Mare Hotel to other regions of the island. Buses run every few hours and are a cost-effective way to travel.

Taxis: Taxis offer convenient and pleasant transportation. You may easily get a taxi from the hotel to your location. The trip from Corfu Mare Hotel to Corfu Town takes only 5 minutes.

Walking: If you prefer to explore the region on foot, Corfu Town is only 2.4 kilometers from the hotel, allowing for a lovely walk.

Car Rentals: Renting a car allows you to explore Corfu at your speed. Car rentals are accessible both at the airport and in Corfu Town.

Bicycle Rentals: For those who prefer cycling, renting a bicycle is an excellent opportunity to view the sites while also getting some exercise.

Contact Address
5 Nikolaou Zervou
Kerkyra, Kerkyra Island, Ionian Islands, Greece 49100
Tel:+30 26610-31011/+30 2661 025804
Fa: 30 26610-25806
Web: corfumare.gr/
Email: info@corfumare.gr

Languages Spoken

- German
- Greek
- English
- French
- Italian
- Albanian

Check-in
From 15:00
Check-out
Until 11:00

Pets
- Pets are not allowed.

Accepted Payment Methods

Maestro, Mastercard, Visa, Diners Club, Cash

2. Divani Corfu Palace

The hotel is located in the verdant woodland area of Kanoni, providing a peaceful setting. It is strategically positioned approximately 3 kilometers from Corfu's town core and 1.5 kilometers from Mon Repos beach, making it simple to visit nearby attractions.

Facilities: The hotel has 162 luxury rooms, two restaurants, a fitness facility, and private parking. It also provides free internet.

Views: Many visitors enjoy the hotel's views, which include the lagoon and the neighboring hills, contributing to the serene atmosphere.

Ratings: The hotel has gotten positive feedback, with an aggregate rating of 4.0, indicating that many customers had good experiences here.

Contact Information

To get more of a personal touch and inquire about specific information or bookings, you can call the Divani Corfu Palace at:

Address: 20, Nafsikas Street, Corfu Town, 49100

Phone: +30 26610 38996

Fax: +30 26610 35 929

Email: info@divanicorfu.gr

Languages Spoken

Greek and English

Check-in	**Check-out**
From 15:00	**Until 11:00**

Age restriction: The minimum age for check-in is 18

3. Siora Vittoria Boutique Hotel

Choosing the Siora Vittoria Boutique Hotel in Corfu for your summer vacation might provide you with a unique and unforgettable experience for various reasons: The hotel is a renovated 19th-century mansion, offering a unique blend of historical elegance and modern luxury.

It's conveniently located in the centre of Corfu's UNESCO Heritage Capital, making it simple to explore the town and its attractions.

The hotel takes pleasure in delivering personalised service, with staff devoted to helping visitors relieve and relax. They provide tailored suggestions for activities and seamless solutions to improve your stay.

Comfort and Amenities

The hotel features 9 beautifully appointed rooms that combine old-world charm with contemporary comforts.

Each room is furnished with custom-made pieces, including Busnelli Adamo armchairs and beds, ensuring a stylish and comfortable environment.

Guests can look forward to an excellent night's sleep thanks to the high-quality pillows and mattresses. The bedding is designed to cradle you to sleep, providing an optimal rest experience.

Every room is equipped with air conditioning, a minibar, and a refrigerator, along with free Wi-Fi access, allowing guests to stay connected and refreshed throughout their stay.

The hotel boasts a flower-filled garden where guests can enjoy moments of peace and tranquility, adding to the serene atmosphere of the boutique hotel.

Complimentary Breakfast: Start your day with a delightful free breakfast, which is included with your stay, offering a variety of choices to suit all tastes.

24-Hour Front Desk and Concierge: The hotel ensures that assistance is always available with a 24-hour front desk and a concierge service, ready to attend to any needs or inquiries you may have.

Contact Information

Address: Stefanou Padova 36, Corfu Town, 49100

Phone: +30 26610 36300

Fax: (+30) 26610 40777
Email: info@SioraVittoria.com

Website: You can visit their official website for more details and reservations.

Check-in   **Check-out**

15:00 - 22:00   07:00 - 11:00

Pets

- Pets are not allowed.

Accepted Payment Methods

Mastercard, Visa, American Express, Cash is not accepted

Child policies

Children of any age are welcome. Children 14 years and above will be charged as adults at this property.

Languages Spoken

- Greek
- English

Attractions Around Siora Vittoria

Here are some nearby attractions and the best ways to explore them:

Corfu Old Town: The atmospheric Old Town is the largest UNESCO site in Greece. Explore its neoclassical buildings, narrow alleyways, antique churches, castles, stone fountains, statues, and monuments. British, French, and Roman influences are evident throughout.

Spianada Square: Visit the postcard-pretty Spianada square, home to the palace of St. Michael & St. George, the municipal art gallery, and the monument of Union of Eptanisa. The Liston Arcade is also nearby.

Old Castle: Explore the imposing Old Castle with the church of St. George. For history buffs and ecclesiastic art lovers, Corfu holds many joys.

Archaeological Museum: Discover exhibits from the 5th and 6th century BC, reflecting the island's ancient history.

Panagia Spiliotissa: Visit this church dating from 1577, showcasing beautiful ecclesiastic art.

Getting Around

Walking: Many attractions are within walking distance of the hotel. Enjoy strolling through the cobblestoned streets and soaking in the historical ambiance.

Bicycle Rentals: The hotel can arrange bicycle rentals, allowing you to explore Corfu Town at your own pace.

Walking Tours: Consider joining walking tours to see the most important places around Corfu Town. The hotel staff can assist with arranging these tours.

4. Eleals Boutique Hotel

Eleals Boutique Hotel is a brand-new luxury hotel that provides unparalleled comfort and top-notch services. It's a haven of luxury and tranquility, encircled by olive trees and situated on a fantastic private beach. The hotel offers breathtaking views of the Ionian Sea, allowing guests to appreciate Corfu's natural beauty in a serene setting.

Modern Amenities
Here are some of the noteworthy comforts and services that make Eleals Boutique Hotel an excellent choice:

The hotel has a variety of accommodation types, including classic, superior, family, and luxury suites. Each room is designed to provide optimum comfort, with amenities like as comfortable beds, couch beds, air conditioning, an extra-long bed, private bathrooms, and walk-in showers. The rooms also include balconies with breathtaking sea or garden views, allowing guests to appreciate the beauty of Corfu straight from their room. On a beautiful private beach, the hotel offers a unique and serene seaside experience. Guests can relax on the beach, swim in the crystal-clear waters of the Ionian Sea, or simply soak up the sun.

Roof Garden: The hotel's roof garden is a standout feature, affording a breathtaking view and inviting guests to repose in its tranquil setting. It's the ideal place to enjoy a variety of excellent food, a cup of coffee, or to relax on the magnificent sunbeds offered.

Guests have frequently commended the hotel's great service, cleanliness, and value, earning it a perfect 5.0 rating based on 189 reviews.

The hotel includes an appealing restaurant and a modern bar where you can relax with your favorite meal or summer drink while taking in the spectacular sea view.

Beautiful Dining: Enjoy a culinary adventure at the hotel's beautiful restaurant. The menu includes a variety of meat and seafood dishes prepared using high-quality ingredients and tasty local goods. The modern bar provides excellent service and cocktails, including amazing signature drinks.

Fitness facility: For guests who want to stay active on vacation, the hotel has a fitness facility with a variety of exercise equipment.

Wifi: During your stay, you'll have complimentary high-speed internet access.

Breakfast: Start your day with a delicious continental breakfast, which is included with your stay.

Parking & Transportation: The hotel offers free private parking, making it convenient for guests who travel with their vehicle.

When staying at the Eleals Boutique Hotel in Corfu, there are various great sights nearby:

Mon Repos Palace: Mon Repos Palace, located about 1.8 miles from the hotel, is a historic site. Explore its stunning grounds and learn about its fascinating history. The palace overlooks the gorgeous Ionian Sea and provides insight into Corfu's past.

Achilleion Palace: Achilleion Palace, located about 0.9 miles away, is another must-see attraction. Empress Elisabeth of Austria (Sisi) erected this neoclassical palace, which has gorgeous architecture, lush gardens, and panoramic views of the Mediterranean.

Museum of Ceramic Art: The Museum of Ceramic Art, located approximately 2.5 miles from the hotel, features stunning ceramic sculptures.

Explore the collection and admire the craftsmanship of local artisans.

Ionio University: located 2.7 miles away, is an important education institution in Corfu. While you're there, you can explore the environs and soak in the local ambiance.

The Serbian Museum: The Serbian Museum is located 2.7 miles from the hotel, and provides insights into Serbia's history and culture. It's a unique attraction worth seeing.

Best Ways to Get Around:

Bus: Take a bus from Corfu to Perama (where the hotel is located).

The bus travel takes about 22 minutes and is a cost-effective method to see the area.

Taxi: You can also take a taxi directly to the Eleals Boutique Hotel. The trip is only 10.6 kilometers, and it's a convenient option.

Walking: If you prefer walking, you can complete the distance by foot. It's around 6.8 kilometers, although walking may take longer.

Here is the contact information for the Eleals Boutique Hotel:

Contact Information
Perama Kerkyras, Corfu 49084, Greece
info@elealshotel.com
(+30) 697 6779492
Phone: +30 2661 041007
Email: info@elealshotel.com

Accepted Payment Methods
Mastercard, Visa, and Cash are not accepted

Check-in	Check-out
14:00 - 22:00	**07:00 - 12:00**

No age restrictions: There is no age minimum for check-in.

Pets are not allowed.

5. Nefeli Hotel

Scenic Location, nestled atop Kommeno's hill, the hotel provides a tranquil and romantic environment, surrounded by a huge garden with olive trees, palm trees, and flowers. It's an ideal location for relaxing.

The hotel has 45 rooms, comprising 21 regular rooms and 24 design rooms, each of which is distinctively furnished with Greek or Corfiot themes and mythology, adding to the charm and experience.

Guests can take advantage of amenities such as a pool with a lawn suitable for lounging, a pool bar for snacks and drinks, an internet corner, a TV corner, safe boxes and a library. Wi-Fi is provided throughout the property.

The hotel is noted for its exceptional service, with staff fluent in Greek, English, German, and French, ensuring a comfortable stay for international customers.

For contact and reservations, the Nefeli Hotel can be reached at:

Address: Dafnila, Kommeno, Corfu, Postal code: 490 83

Phone: +30 2661 091033

Email: info@hotelnefeli.com

Check-in   **Check-out**

From 15:00   Until 11:00

No age restriction: There is no age requirement for check-in

Pets

- Pets are allowed. Charges may be applicable.

Accepted Payment Methods

Mastercard, Visa, Cash is not accepted

Interesting Attractions Near The Nefeli Hotel That You Might Enjoy:

Aqualand Park Corfu: This water park, located just a short drive from the hotel, provides enjoyment for the entire family with a range of slides and pools.

Ypapanti Church: This church, located within an 8-minute walk from the hotel, is a lovely spot to visit.

Dafnila Beach: A 20-minute walk from the hotel, this little beach is ideal for a day of leisure.

Capodistrias Museum: This museum, located 3.5 kilometers from the hotel, is dedicated to Ioannis Kapodistrias, Greece's first governor.

The Old Fortress (Citadel): Built by the Venetians in 1546 on the site of an ancient castle. It is located on a tiny rocky peninsula east of the old town. It provides breathtaking views of Corfu Town and the brilliant turquoise waters of the Ionian Sea. Don't miss the modest chapel inside, designed in the form of a Doric temple, and the lighthouse at the top.

The Esplanade (Spianada): Is Europe's second-largest square, boasting immense green space. It's a popular site for both locals and visitors. Enjoy the arcaded Liston, which was built by the French in the nineteenth century and features cafes great for people watching. Locals even play cricket on the well-kept lawns.

New Fortress: The Venetians built the huge New Fortress in 1577 to safeguard the city from the Turks, which may be reached via an uphill trek past the open market. Explore the fortifications and take in panoramic views of Corfu Town and the sea towards Albania.

Church of St. Spyridon (Áyios Spyrídon): Visit the iconic Church of St. Spyridon (Áyios Spyrídon), devoted to Corfu's patron saint. Its bell tower dominates the horizon, and the inside retains the remnants of St. Spyridon. The church is an important pilgrimage site for both locals and tourists.

Mon Repos: Explore the lovely Mon Repos estate and its neoclassical mansion, established as a summer residence for the British Lord High Commissioner and subsequently became the birthplace of Prince Philip, Duke of Edinburgh. The surrounding grounds are ideal for a leisurely stroll.

The Church of Saints Jason and Sosipater: Discover this historic church from the eleventh century. It is dedicated to Saints Jason and Sosipater,

Corfu's patron saints. The church has Byzantine-style architecture and stunning artwork.

Exploring the region surrounding the Nefeli Hotel in Corfu and its adjacent attractions is pretty simple. Here are some transit alternatives and suggestions for getting around:

Bus: KTEL Kerkyras operates a local bus service from Kommeno to Corfu every three hours. The ride takes about 16 minutes and is an inexpensive way to get to Corfu Town and other local sites.

Taxis: Taxis are easily accessible and might provide a speedy means to travel from the hotel to nearby destinations. A cab ride from Nefeli Hotel to Corfu Town takes roughly 14 minutes and covers a distance of 12.9 kilometers, costing between €24 and €30.

Car rental: Car rental allows you to explore Corfu at your own leisure. You can explore far-flung attractions and take gorgeous drives around the island.

Walking: Walking to neighboring sights might be a relaxing way to explore. The The surrounding area of the hotel is beautiful, and many sites are within a reasonable walking distance.

Excursion Boats: For attractions along the coast or on the water, consider taking an excursion boat. This is a great way to see Corfu from a different perspective and visit beaches or coastal landmarks.

6. The Royal Hotel

The Royal Hotel is a three-star establishment located in the heart of Corfu Island, overlooking Kanoni Bay. It's set in a historic location renowned for its rich cultural history, excellent food, and outstanding views. The hotel is just five minutes from the historic center and is surrounded by sightseeing miracles, making it an ideal choice for those looking to immerse themselves in the relaxing atmosphere of a warm and comfortable historical building.

Amenities and Services:

The hotel has 136 luxury rooms and suites, providing a variety of options to suit your needs.

Guests can enjoy free parking and internet access, which will make their stay more convenient.

A large pool and a seawater-filled children's pool are available for relaxing.

Dining options include one restaurant, one bar, and one cafeteria, all of which have a gorgeous patio overlooking Mouse Island. The hotel features modern decor, outstanding service, and customized attention to detail.

Check-in Time: Guests can check in whenever it is most convenient for them, as the hotel is flexible enough to suit varied travel plans.

Languages Spoken:

The staff at the Royal Hotel are multilingual, speaking English, French, German, and Greek, catering to a diverse international clientele.

Pets

Pet-friendly

Location and Contact

Palaiopolis 110, Kanoni, Corfu Greece, 49100.

Tel: +30 26610 353

Email: reservations@royalgrandhotel.gr.

Nearby Attractions:

- Vlacherna Monastery, located 0.2 miles away, provides a spiritual refuge and historical insight.
- Mouse Island, a short boat ride away, is known for its scenic views and the 11th-century Byzantine chapel of Pantokrator.
- Kanoni Causeway and Harbour are within walking distance, ideal for picturesque walks and sea breezes.

Transportation Options:

- Local bus service is a cost-effective option to travel to Corfu Town and other attractions.

- Taxis: Taxis provide a quick transfer to your location and are easily accessible from the hotel.
- Car Rental: Renting a car allows you to explore the island at your speed.
- Excursion Boats: Take a boat cruise to discover coastal features and nearby islands.

7. Ariti Grand Hotel

The Ariti Grand Hotel is a four-star hotel in Kanoni, about 3.5 kilometers from Corfu Town. It is encircled by a 4000m2 garden and provides amazing views of the lagoon, the airport, and a portion of Corfu town. The hotel's lounge area extends onto a spacious terrace, ideal for watching the breathtaking Ionian lagoon sunset.

Amenities and Service

The hotel has 156 air-conditioned rooms with refrigerators and Select Comfort beds outfitted with Egyptian cotton sheets. Guests can enjoy two swimming pools, one with a children's section, as well as free WiFi throughout the hotel. Dining options include a restaurant, a main bar, and a pool bar.

Check-In Time: Guests can check in at their convenience, as the reception is open 24/7.

Language Spoken

The Ariti Grand Hotel's multilingual staff speaks English, German, and Greek, serving an international customer.

Contact Address:

Address: Nafsikas 41, Kanoni Corfu, 49100, Greece

Phone: +30 26610 33885

Email: info@aritihotelcorfu.com

Pet and Child Policy: The hotel's pool includes a children's section, showing that it is a family-friendly setting. However, pets are not permitted.

Nearby Attractions

Vlacherna Monastery and Mouse Island, provide both cultural and scenic experiences.

Paleopoli (Corfu's Old Town) and gorgeous beaches like as Mon Repos and Garitsa are also nearby.

Transportation Options:

A bus stop is conveniently located right across the street, providing easy access to Corfu Town and other attractions.

Taxis are readily available for quick transfers to various destinations.

8. Aegli Hotel

The family-run Aegli Hotel, located 5 kilometers from Benitses Beach, provides air-conditioned rooms with views of Pontikonisi Island. The resort, set in a lush garden, includes a snack bar and a children's playground, as well as its private beach.

Aegli's rooms are tastefully decorated with warm tones and dark timber accents. Everyone owns a phone, a refrigerator, and a television. The majority of units feature a furnished balcony with unobstructed views of the Ionian Sea. Guests can start their day with a breakfast buffet in the dining area. The on-site snack bar serves drinks, ouzo, light snacks, and fresh juices all day.

The staff at the front desk can assist with bicycle and car rental arrangements, as well as provide childcare services upon request. The hotel's common spaces have complimentary WiFi. It is possible to walk to the Agia Kiriaki and Vlacherena Medieval Monasteries. The Aegli Hotel is located 4 kilometers from Achilleion Palace and 7 km from Corfu Town and Port. Palaiokastritsa Village is separated by 30 km. On-site private parking is free.

Check-in   **Check-out**
14:00 - 00:00   **08:00 - 12:00**

No age restriction: There is no age requirement for check-in

Pets
- Pets are not allowed.

Accepted Payment Methods
Mastercard, Visa, Cash.

Contact Information

Address: Perama Gastouriou, Perama 49084, 490 84, Greece

Phone: +30 2661 043000 / +306979308356

Email: reservations@royalgrandhotel.gr / reservations@royalgrandhotel.gr

9.Delfino Blu Boutique Hotel

This boutique hotel in Corfu was built amphitheatrically and overlooks the beach at Agios Stephanos. It features well-lit studios equipped with DVD players, LCD televisions, and computers. There are two bars and two swimming pools on site. Every studio at the Delfino Blu is airy and spacious, with a private balcony that overlooks the sea. Each features a spacious sitting space with a sofa and a modern bathroom with a Jacuzzi bathtub. Guests at the à la carte restaurant Kohili can enjoy a romantic evening on the open-air terrace under the stars, with a spectacular view of the small islands and the sunset.

The pool bar La Veranda is located next to the pool, beneath the rocky waterfalls. It serves small appetizers and pleasant drinks.

Under the strains of Latin music, the beach bar Mango serves up fresh salads and grills. Nestled near the vibrant nightlife of Sidari, but far enough away from the bustling Corfu, lies the serene haven of Delfino Blu.

Languages spoken
- German
- Greek
- English

Check-in   **Check-out**

15:00 - 00:00   08:00 - 11:00

The reception is open from 8:00 until 24:00, providing flexibility for guests upon arrival and departure

No age restriction: There is no age requirement for check-in

Pets
- Pets are not allowed.

Accepted Payment Methods

Maestro, Mastercard, Visa, Diners Club, Cash

Address and Contact
Corfu, Agios Stefanos 490 81, Greece

Tel: +30 26630 51629, +30 26630 51628, +30 6973 623514

Email: info@delfinoblu.gr

Attraction Area Nearby the Hotel

- Agios Stefanos Beach: A short walk from the hotel, this beach has golden sand, and blue shallow seas, and is considered quite safe for families with children.
- Elisabeth's Gift & Jewellery Shop is located around 0.2 kilometers from the hotel and offers unique souvenirs and presents.
- Little Agios Stefanos Church: A lovely holy site located around 0.2 miles away.
- Perditas Glass Art: For art connoisseurs, this specialized shop is a must-see and is conveniently located near the hotel.

How to Explore:

- On Foot: Many of these attractions are easily accessible by foot.
- Car Rental: The Delfino Blu Boutique Hotel offers car rental services for those looking to explore Corfu. This allows you to explore more distant attractions at your speed.
- Cab: For convenience, consider taking a cab to distant sites.

- Bus: A bus station is located 50 meters from the hotel, and green buses are available for transit across the island.

BUDGET ACCOMMODATIONS

1. Konstantinoupolis Hotel

The Konstantinoupolis Hotel is a historic hotel set in a restored 19th-century building in the heart of Corfu town, full of beauty and with a warm authentic family feel, and offers a panoramic view of the sea and the islets of Vido and Lazaretto. It distinguishes itself by providing good value for money while also providing exquisite Greek hospitality.

Amenities and Service:

The hotel has 31 rooms, each with individual air conditioning, a flat-screen TV, a hairdryer, a mini-fridge, and free WiFi. Guests may take advantage of a 24-hour front desk, speedy check-in and out, and baggage storage. There is also a snack bar with light meals and snacks.

Check-In Time: Guests can check in at their convenience, as the reception is open 24 hours.

Languages Spoken: The hotel's multilingual staff speaks Greek, English, and maybe other languages, and serves a wide international customer.

Location and Address:

Address: K. Zabitsianou 11, Corfu Town, 49100, Greece.

Nearby Attractions:

The hotel is less than a minute's walk from the famed Spianada Square, as well as the Old Fortress, Corfu Archaeological Museum, and Antivouniotissa Byzantine Museum.

Transportation Options

For getting around, there is a municipal parking area located just opposite the hotel for easy access.

You can explore Corfu Town on foot, ride local buses to famous resorts, rent a car, scooter, or ATV for more flexibility, or take a cab to get to your destination quickly.

Dining options near the Konstantinoupolis Hotel in Corfu:

Avli: is a Greek traditional restaurant located near Alk. Darri & Athin. Kavvada. It provides a paradise of flavors, presenting you with the mysteries of Greek cuisine. Highly recommended for a taste of traditional Greek flavors.

Arcadion Bistrot: located at 44 Kapodistriou Str., Liston, Corfu Town, provides excellent service and food in a beautiful environment. Don't miss the breathtaking vistas while dining.

Psaraki: located at 34 Kapodistriou Str, Pentofanaro Square, Corfu Town, serves fish. Enjoy fresh fish dishes and a variety of Greek marine flavors.

A Mano: This Italian restaurant at Gerasimou Prifti 15 serves Neapolitan and Campanian food. Ideal for pizza lovers and those who enjoy Italian cuisine.

Lampadina Traditional Cuisine: Located at Gerasimou Prifti 19, this restaurant offers delicious Greek and Mediterranean fare. A fantastic spot to sample local flavors.

Alatopipero: Located at Dona 17 Prosalendou 16, this restaurant serves Greek and Mediterranean dishes.

Bakalogatos: Located at Alipiou 23 Prosalendou, serves Mediterranean and Greek meals. A fantastic option for a satisfying meal.

Tabule Rasa: Located at Dona 9, serves quick food, Mediterranean, Greek, and Middle Eastern cuisine. Enjoy wonderful meals and courteous service.

Agioli Restaurant: Located in Nikiforou Theotoki 128, this restaurant serves seafood, Mediterranean, and Greek cuisine. Try the wonderful vegetarian meze.

Lasmari Apraos Restaurant: Although not directly near the hotel, this restaurant is worth mentioning.

Situated between Kassiopi and Achravi Str, it offers fabulous food, quick service, and friendly staff.

2. Pergamos Village

Pergamos Village is situated among palm trees and flowers, creating a peaceful and scenic setting. The house has stone-covered floors and built-in sofas, which enhance the aesthetic appeal and comfort of your stay.

Pergamos Village in Corfu is a wonderful accommodation option that provides a variety of amenities and services to ensure a pleasant and relaxing stay. Here is a thorough overview:

Amenities and Services:

Outdoor Pool: A lovely outdoor pool with a separate children's area, ideal for relaxation and entertainment.

Snack Bar: Provides a selection of snacks and drinks to enjoy by the pool.

Free Wi-Fi: Stay connected with free internet access in public spaces.

Self-Catered Accommodation: Spacious studios and apartments with kitchenettes for your convenience.

Garden and Sea Views: From your balcony, you can enjoy calm views of the garden, pool, or the Cretan Sea.

English Breakfast: Begin the day with a hearty English breakfast served on the property.

Contact and Address:

Pergamos Village is located in Chania, Kolymvari, 73006, Greece.

Phone Number: You can contact them on 2824 022944 for more information.

Languages Spoken:

The staff at Pergamos Village are proficient in English and Greek, ensuring smooth communication during your stay.

Nearby Attractions:

Rapaniana Beach: Take a short walk to the beach and enjoy the sun and sea.

Chania Town: Visit the famous lighthouse and other town attractions, which are a short drive away.

Cave of St John the Hermit: For those interested in historical sites, this cave is a short distance away from the village.

Transportation:

Car Rental: The staff can assist you with car rentals to explore the island at your own pace.

Public Buses: Utilize the local bus service to move around the island conveniently.

Taxis: Taxis are readily available for easy and fast transfers to your destinations.

To get from Corfu Airport (CFU) to Pergamos Village, you can follow these general directions:

Exit the airport and head towards E.O. Aerodromiou Peleka.

Follow E.O. Aerodromiou Peleka for a short distance.

Take the route towards E.O. Kerkiras Achiliou.

Continue on E.O. Kerkiras Achiliou until you reach the area of Kolymvari, where Pergamos Village is located.

The journey is relatively straightforward and should take approximately 30 minutes by car, depending on traffic. It's always a good idea to check a navigation app like Google Maps or MapQuest for live directions and traffic updates to ensure the smoothest trip possible.

If you prefer not to drive, there are other options such as taking a taxi directly from the airport or using the local bus service. The staff at Pergamos Village can also assist with transportation arrangements if needed. Enjoy your trip to Corfu!

3. Piccolo Centrale

Piccolo Centrale in Corfu provides a lovely stay with its deliberately designed spaces and handy position in the heart of Corfu Town, Greece. Piccolo Centrale provides magnificent city views as well as views of the inner courtyard, which add to the ambiance.

Facility Description:

The unit is 431 ft², offering adequate space for visitors. It has a separate bedroom, living room, fully equipped kitchen with dining area, and a private bathroom. The flat is air-conditioned, ensuring a comfortable stay whatever the weather. The inside is elegantly decorated, with a clean and contemporary look. Guests have commented that the unit is immaculately clean.

Kitchen amenities include modern appliances such as an oven, microwave, and coffee machine. The apartment is allergy-free and accommodates guests with sensitivity.

Services

Free WiFi is accessible throughout the hotel, allowing you to stay connected at all times.

Parking: Free parking is available, which is a major advantage for people traveling by car.

Convenience: The facility has luggage storage and an ATM, making your stay more convenient.

Host Interaction: The hosts are complimented for being good and friendly, frequently interacting via WhatsApp to address any needs or inquiries.

Additional Amenities:

The apartment includes a washing machine, making it ideal for extended stays. It is a non-smoking facility, creating a comfortable environment for all guests.

Guest Experience: Visitors have consistently rated their experience as exceptional, highlighting the wonderful host, excellent location, and cozy, well-appointed apartment.

Nearby Restaurants And Cafes That Are Worth Visiting

Piccolo Espresso Bar

Address: Καποδιστρίου 66, Aiyaleo, Attiki, 122 41.

Hours: Open daily from 11:30 AM to 11:00 PM.

Phone: 2661 039649.

Monte Cafe: Known for its European cuisine and cozy atmosphere.

Favela 17: Offers delicious pancakes and flavorful coffee.

Tomateli: A hidden gem with a traditional yard and Mediterranean flavors

Nearby Attractions:

- Saint Spyridon Church is just a two-minute walk away.
- Serbian Museum is a four-minute walk from the flat.
- Municipal Gallery is 500 yards away.
- New Fortress and Port of Corfu: Also nearby.

Transportation:

- Corfu International Airport is about 2.5 miles away, making it handy for air travelers.
- Public transportation: Local buses (blue and green lines) travel small distances and link to various regions of the island.
- Taxis are readily available around tourist destinations, ports, and the airport.
- Car rentals are an alternative for people who want to explore at their own pace.

Address:

Piccolo Centrale, Νικηφόρου Θεοτόκη, Corfu Town, 49100, Greece

Check-in and Out Policies

Early Check-In: Check-in at Piccolo Centrale is from 15:00 onwards. Late Check-Out: Guests must check out by 11:00. If you require an early check-in or a late check-out, it's recommended to contact the property directly to make arrangements. The hosts are known for their helpfulness and may accommodate your request depending on availability.

4. Hotel Zeus

Hotel Zeus in Corfu, also known as Zeus Throne Suites, provides a magnificent and pleasant stay with a variety of amenities and services designed to meet the demands of its visitors. It is surrounded by the island's natural splendor.

The facility's rooms have stunning sea views from their clifftop location. It was recently remodeled, creating a modern and stylish environment.

Amenities:

Infinity Pool: A breathtaking infinity pool with spectacular ocean views.

Air-conditioned suites include a lounge area and a flat-screen TV with streaming options.

Suites have a kitchen with an oven, refrigerator, hob, coffee machine, and kettle.

Private bathrooms are modern and have a walk-in shower, bathrobes, and slippers.

Complimentary Additions: Guests are received with wine or champagne, fruits, and chocolates or cookies.

Services:

Breakfast Options: Guests can enjoy both à la carte and continental breakfasts, which include heated dishes, local delicacies, and fresh pastries.

Free WiFi provides high-speed internet access throughout the hotel.

Private Parking: Guests can park conveniently on-site.

Airport Shuttle: Provides convenient transportation to and from the hotel.

Contact and Address:

Location: Afionas B1, Afionas, 49081, Greece

Phone: 0030 2663051311.

Email: Contact through the official website.

Language Spoken:

English: The staff at Zeus Throne Suites are proficient in English, ensuring smooth communication with international guests.

Check-In Time: Usually after 2:00 PM.

Check-Out Time: Typically by 11:00 AM

Nearby Attractions:

Porto Timoni Beach: A stunning beach located close to the suites.

Agios Georgios Beach: Another beautiful beach in proximity.

Transportation:

Private Parking: Available on-site for guests traveling by car.

Airport Shuttle: For convenient travel to and from the airport.

Several surrounding restaurants and cafés offer a great dining experience with breathtaking views and delicious cuisine.

- **Zeus Throne Restaurant:**

Hotel Zeus offers a delightful dining experience with its on-site restaurant, Zeus Throne Restaurant. The restaurant serves exquisite Greek cuisine with a menu featuring local vegetables and ingredients. Guests can enjoy their meals while taking in the picturesque sea view above St George Bay and the enchanting atmosphere by night.

- **Dionysos Restaurant**

Cuisine: Mediterranean, Greek, and European. It is conveniently located approximately 0 kilometers from the Zeus Throne Resort.

- **Porto Timoni Restaurant Cafe**

Porto Timoni Restaurant Cafe serves Mediterranean and Greek cuisine. 0 miles from Zeus Throne Resort, ideal for a lunch with a view.

- **Anemos Taverna**

Anemos Taverna serves Mediterranean/Greek cuisine. Only 0.1 mile from Zeus Throne Resort.

- **The Grill**

The Grill offers a variety of cuisine options, including steakhouses, cafes, Greek, diners, and beer restaurants. A short stroll of 0.1 mile from the resort.

- **Luuma Restaurant with a View**

Cuisines: Italian and Greek. Only 0.1 kilometers away, with stunning scenery and a fantastic mood.

Here are some nearby attractions to help travelers make the most of their holiday.

Porto Timoni Beach: A lovely double-sided beach near Afionas with pristine seas and wonderful views.

Agios Georgios Beach: is a long sandy beach with crystal clear waters, perfect for swimming and sunbathing.

Angelokastro: A Byzantine fortress with magnificent views of the island and sea.

Arillas Beach: A calm beach with a relaxed environment, ideal for families.

Corfu Donkey Rescue: A sanctuary for donkeys where visitors can interact with these gentle animals.

The Vine: A popular spot for nightlife, offering a selection of drinks and entertainment.

Anemomilos Windmill: A historic windmill that now houses a cafe and restaurant with stunning coastal views.

5. History House Corfu

History House is a newly restored condo hotel that combines old elegance with modern comforts. The house is recognized for its cleanliness, comfort, and prime location on the outskirts of the ancient town, making it a great choice for those looking to discover Corfu's rich history and vibrant culture.

Amenities and Services:

Air-conditioned rooms: Ensure your comfort during your stay.

Private bathrooms are equipped with a hairdryer and free toiletries.

Connectivity: Free WiFi is available throughout the facility. Each room has a flat-screen television and a safety deposit box.

Beverage facilities include a coffee machine in each room.

Views: Some rooms have balconies and give garden views.

Garden: A place to unwind and enjoy the outdoors.

Services:

Help yourself. Breakfast: A kitchen is accessible, with a diverse assortment of breakfast foods.

The home and apartments are kept immaculately clean, including a lovely patio for guests to relax on.

Staff: The staff are praised for their friendliness and helpfulness.

Contact and Address:

3 Vrela Armeni, Corfu Town, 49100, Greece

Nearby Attractions:

Asian Art Museum: A diverse collection of Asian art is just a short walk away.

Serbian Museum: Discover historical treasures around the property.

Panagia Vlahernon Church: is a neighboring religious and architectural landmark.

Old Fortress: A historical site that provides insights into Corfu's past.

Exploring The Area

On Foot: Many attractions are within walking distance due to the central location.

Public Buses: Blue city buses and green intercity buses connect you to various parts of the island.

Taxis: Readily available near tourist spots for convenient travel.

Car Rentals: An option for those who prefer to explore at their own pace.

Breakfast Options Provided By History House Corfu

History House Corfu provides a "help yourself" breakfast in the kitchen, with a diverse selection of breakfast foods for visitors to enjoy. The kitchen is located in a separate area of the structure, accessible via the garden. Guests can select from a variety of alternatives and customize their breakfast.

For more particular information on the sorts of meals available or any dietary accommodations, please contact

History House Corfu directly where you want to make your reservation. Breakfast in the garden is a great way to start the day in Corfu.

For meals beyond breakfast, guests can explore the local area, which is rich in culinary offerings. Here are some recommended nearby options:

Old Times

A restaurant that offers takeaway, outside seating, and alcohol. It's an excellent choice for a casual lunch or a drink.

Il Pirata

This restaurant, located just a 5-minute walk from the History House, serves Greek cuisine and is a favorite choice among guests.

Given History House's strategic location in Corfu Town, there are numerous restaurants and pubs within walking distance that cater to a variety of tastes and interests. For the most up-to-date and precise recommendations, ask the staff at History House when you arrive, as they are likely to have the most recent information on the greatest local sites.

6. Loc Aparthotel Annunziata

Loc Aparthotel Annunziata in Corfu is a great choice for vacation accommodation due to its comprehensive amenities, convenient location, and the services it offers. Here's a detailed overview:

Amenities and Services:

Air-conditioned rooms with microwaves and smart televisions provide a comfortable stay.

Connectivity: Free WiFi is available throughout the facility.

Kitchenette: Complete with a microwave, dining area, refrigerator, stovetop, toaster, and kettle.

Private bathrooms provide showers and hair dryers for your comfort.

Entertainment: Flat-screen televisions with streaming services.

Additional Services: Airport transfers, bicycle rentals, tourist tours, and vehicle rentals are offered.

Contact and Address:

Agion Pateron 22, Corfu Town, 49100, Greece.

Phone: 694 937 0971.

Languages Spoken:

English, German, and Greek are spoken at the aparthotel, ensuring good communication with international guests.

Nearby Attractions:

Serbian Museum: Only 300 meters away.

Municipal Gallery and New Fortress: Also nearby.

Asian Art Museum is a short distance from the site.

Anemomilos Windmill: A historic windmill that currently houses a cafe and restaurant with breathtaking beach views.

Transportation Options:

Airport Proximity: Corfu International Airport is only 2 kilometers away, with airport shuttles provided by the accommodation.

Exploring the Area: You can rent a bicycle or a car from the aparthotel, or join neighborhood cycling and bar crawls.

Restaurant and bar in Loc Aparthotel Annunziata Corfu's

Loc Aparthotel Annunziata provides a unique urban living experience with close dining options. The hotel does not have an in-house restaurant or bar. However, due to its prominent location in Corfu's historical center, guests may easily walk to a variety of local cafes and bars. Here are some possibilities to consider:

Urban Suites by LOC Hospitality:

Offers beautifully renovated studio suites with kitchenettes, allowing guests to prepare their meals if desired.

Nearby Dining

The area is rich with local cafes, tavernas, and restaurants where guests can enjoy traditional Greek cuisine and international dishes.

Beach and City Vibes

In less than 10 minutes on a bike or walking, guests can reach the sea and enjoy the beaches where they can find beachside restaurants and bars to relax and dine.

CHAPTER THREE

Attractions and Activities

Must- Visit Landmarks and Attractions in Corfu

Corfu, famed for its rich history, cultural legacy, and natural beauty, has a treasure mine of landmarks and attractions that draw travelers from all over the world. Corfu's must-see attractions range from ancient ruins and historic sites to magnificent mansions and estates, offering insights into the island's history, architecture, and cultural significance. In this guide, we'll look at three prominent landmarks in Corfu that are must-sees for tourists looking to immerse themselves in the island's history, beauty, and charm.

1. Old Town Corfu

Old Town Corfu, a UNESCO World Heritage Site, is a historic jewel located on Corfu Island's eastern shore. Old Town Corfu, with its Venetian architecture, narrow cobblestone alleyways, and old defenses, transports visitors back to a time of medieval splendor and marine influence.

Must-See Attractions

a) Liston Promenade
The Liston Promenade, inspired by Paris' Rue de Rivoli, is a lovely cobblestone strip surrounded by exquisite cafés, arcades, and Venetian-style houses.
Visitors can take strolls, people-watch, and sample traditional Corfiot food on the outdoor terraces.

b) Old Fortress (Palaio Frourio)
The Old Fortress, located on a rocky peninsula facing the Ionian Sea, is a historic fortification dating back to the Byzantine era. Highlights include the Venetian walls of British barracks, panoramic views from the clock tower, and exhibitions at the fortress museum.

c) New Fortress (neo-Frourio)
The New Fortress, built during the Venetian period to protect Corfu Town from Ottoman attacks, boasts spectacular defenses, subterranean tunnels, a lighthouse, and breathtaking views of the town, harbor, and surrounding sea.

d) Saint Spyridon Church
Saint Spyridon Church, dedicated to Corfu's patron saint, is a Byzantine-style landmark with a bell tower, elaborate murals, saint's relics, and liturgical events reflecting the island's Orthodox Christian background.

e) Corfu Archaeological Museum

The Corfu Historic Museum, housed in a neoclassical edifice, contains a large collection of artifacts, sculptures, pottery, and inscriptions from ancient Corfu, including exhibits from the Temple of Artemis and other historic sites.

Activities

• **Walking Tours:** Explore Old Town Corfu on guided walking tours that showcase its historic sites, architectural marvels, hidden alleys, and local legends.

• **Shopping:** Browse artisan shops, boutiques, and craft markets in Old Town Corfu for handmade souvenirs, jewelry, ceramics, olive wood products, and local delicacies.

• **Cultural Events:** Attend cultural events, festivals, and concerts held in Old Town Corfu's squares, theaters, and cultural venues, celebrating music, dance, and traditional arts.

-

2. Achilleon Palace

Achilleion Palace, a neoclassical house in the town of Gastouri, south of Corfu Town, stands as a witness to the island's imperial history. Achilleion Palace, built in the late nineteenth century as a summer residence for Empress Elisabeth of Austria (Sisi), is well-known for its sumptuous architecture, lush gardens, and panoramic views of the Ionian Sea.

Must-See Attractions

a. Grand Staircases and Statues
The magnificent staircase of Achilleion Palace displays majestic statues of Achilles, the mythical Greek hero, and other mythological figures, symbolizing strength, beauty, and heroic ideals.

b. Empress Sisi's rooms
Visitors can tour Empress Sisi's magnificent apartments, such as the Throne Room, Music Room, and Empress's Bedroom, which are decorated with beautiful paintings, chandeliers, period furniture, and the empress' items.

c. Gardens of Achilleion
Achilleion Palace's landscaped grounds have quiet walks, statues, fountains, and panoramic terraces overlooking the sea, resulting in a peaceful getaway complete with Mediterranean flora, sculptures, and shaded spots for leisure.

d. Achilles Dying Statue
Achilleion's gardens are centered around the famed statue of Achilles Dying, which depicts the wounded hero in a sorrowful and dramatic stance, surrounded by rich flora and picturesque surroundings.

Activities

• Take guided tours of Achilleion Palace to learn about its history, architecture, and relationship to Empress Elisabeth. Gain insights into the palace's design, symbolism, and restoration process.
• Take a stroll around Achilleion's palace grounds to admire statues, enjoy panoramic views, and rest in the peaceful outdoor settings.
• Take photos of Achilleion Palace's interiors, exteriors, gardens, statues, and picturesque views to preserve memories of this architectural masterpiece.

3. Mon Repos Estate

Mon Repos Estate, near Corfu Town, is a historic estate renowned for its neoclassical mansion, rich gardens, and archeological monuments. Originally constructed as a summer residence for the British Lord High Commissioner, Mon Repos is today a public park and cultural landmark with botanical gardens, walking trails, and historical significance.

Must-See Attractions

a. Mon Repos Villa
Mon Repos' neoclassical villa boasts magnificent architecture, period furnishings, art collections, and

displays commemorating the estate's history, residents, and cultural legacy.

b. Botanical Gardens
Mon Repos Estate's botanical gardens feature a rich assortment of plants, trees, flowers, and native vegetation, creating a picturesque backdrop for leisurely walks, picnics, and nature appreciation.

c. Archaeological sites
Explore the ancient ruins and archeological sites on Mon Repos Estate, which include the remnants of a Roman villa, ancient baths, Byzantine structures, and historical objects discovered during excavations.

d. Seaside views
Mon Repos Estate's coastline trails offer panoramic views of the Ionian Sea, coastal cliffs, rocky coves, and natural landscapes that inspire rest and exploration.

Activities

- **Historical Tours**: Join guided tours of Mon Repos Estate to learn about its historical significance, architectural features, botanical diversity, and archaeological discoveries.
- **Nature Walks**: Take leisurely walks through the botanical gardens, coastal trails, and shaded

pathways of Mon Repos, spotting wildlife, birds, and Mediterranean flora along the way.

- **Picnics and Relaxation**: Enjoy picnics, outdoor activities, and relaxation in the tranquil settings of Mon Repos Estate, surrounded by nature, history, and scenic beauty.

Museums and Cultural Sites in Corfu: A Journey Through History and Art

Corfu is home to a diverse network of museums and cultural attractions that provide insights into its interesting past and artistic legacy. Corfu's museums include ancient relics, Byzantine treasures, and Asian art collections, highlighting the varied influences and contributions that have influenced the island's identity throughout the years. On this trip, we'll visit three major museums in Corfu: the Archaeological Museum, the Byzantine Museum, and the Asian Art Museum. We'll talk about their collections, their relevance, and the immersive experiences they provide to visitors looking to uncover Corfu's cultural treasures.

Archaeological Museum of Corfu

History & Collections

The Archeological Museum of Corfu, located in the heart of Corfu Town, includes an extensive collection of archeological artifacts spanning thousands of years, from prehistoric times to the Roman era. The museum's holdings highlight the island's ancient civilizations, including objects from the Greek, Roman, and Byzantine periods, as well as discoveries from excavations in Corfu and the surrounding area.

Highlights and exhibits

1. Prehistoric objects: The museum exhibits Neolithic, Bronze Age, and Iron Age objects, such as pottery, tools, and figures, providing insight into the island's early settlements and cultural development.
2. Greek and Roman Sculptures: Visitors can admire marble sculptures, statues, and reliefs depicting mythological figures, deities, and historical personalities from ancient Greece and Rome,

showcasing the artistic achievements of the classical period.

3. Mosaic Floors and Inscriptions: The museum showcases ancient Corfu's mosaic floors, inscriptions, and architectural remains, emphasizing their artistry, symbolism, and historical significance.

4. Byzantine and Christian Art: The museum exhibits icons, religious objects, and frescoes depicting the island's Byzantine origins and spiritual traditions.

Experiences and Recommendations

• **Guided Tour:** Explore the Archaeological Museum's exhibits, learn about Corfu's ancient past, and appreciate the significance of each artifact in the island's cultural growth.

• **Interactive exhibitions**, multimedia displays, and educational materials offer detailed explanations, historical context, and engaging experiences for visitors of all ages.

• **Special exhibitions:** Check for special exhibitions, temporary displays, and cultural events hosted by the museum, featuring guest curators, themed collections, and collaborations with international institutions to enhance the visitor experience.

• **Educational Programs:** The museum offers educational programs, workshops, and activities for schools, families, and tourists, including hands-on archaeology workshops, guided tours for children, and cultural workshops on ancient crafts and techniques.

Byzantine Museum of Corfu

History & Collections

The Byzantine Museum of Corfu is committed to conserving and displaying the island's Byzantine heritage, religious art, and cultural legacy. The museum's treasures, housed in a historic structure near the Old Fortress, include icons, frescoes, manuscripts, and religious artifacts from the Byzantine to post-Byzantine periods.

Highlights and exhibits

1. The museum's iconography collection includes works by renowned artists, religious subjects, and stylistic variants reflecting Byzantine spiritual and creative traditions from centuries ago.
2. Replicas of Byzantine frescoes from Corfu's churches and monasteries showcase iconography, religious storytelling, and mural painting techniques.
3. Religious Artifacts: The museum displays religious artifacts, liturgical objects, and ecclesiastical items used in Byzantine worship, including chalices, vestments, crosses, and religious manuscripts.

4. Historical Context: Exhibits provide historical context, interpretive panels, and multimedia presentations that elucidate the significance of Byzantine art, architecture, and spirituality in Corfu's cultural and religious landscape.

Experiences and Recommendations

• **Icon Workshop:** Participate in an icon painting workshop or demonstration organized by the museum, where skilled artisans share techniques, symbolism, and spiritual significance of Byzantine iconography.

• **Guided Tour:** Join a guided tour of the Byzantine Museum to explore its collections, learn about Byzantine art and history, and gain insights into the religious and cultural context of the icons and artifacts on display.

• **Lecture Series:** Attend lectures, seminars, and scholarly talks hosted by the museum, featuring experts in Byzantine studies, art history, and religious iconography who provide in-depth analyses and interpretations of the museum's collections.

• **Virtual Tours:** Explore virtual tours or online exhibits offered by the museum, allowing visitors to experience Byzantine art and culture from anywhere in the world through interactive digital platforms and multimedia resources.

Asian Art Museum in Corfu

History & Collections

The Asian Art Museum of Corfu is a hidden gem that honors the island's historic ties to Asia by displaying a diverse collection of art, antiquities, and cultural objects from East and Southeast Asia. The museum, housed in a historic building near the Liston Promenade, has collections of ceramics, textiles, sculptures, paintings, and decorative arts from China, Japan, India, and other countries.

Highlights and exhibits

1. Chinese Porcelain: The museum's collection includes Ming and Qing period ceramics, blue-and-white ware, Famille rose, and export porcelain, reflecting China's artistic traditions and trade history.

2. Japanese Prints and Paintings: Visitors can view woodblock prints, ukiyo-e paintings, and traditional artworks featuring landscapes, kabuki theater, geisha, and samurai culture, showcasing Japan's artistic heritage and craftsmanship.

3. Indian Textiles and Sculptures: The museum displays Indian textiles, fabrics, and sculptures, including silk sarees, embroidered textiles, and religious sculptures that highlight India's diverse cultural traditions and craftsmanship.

4. Southeast Asian Art: Exhibits include artworks and artifacts from Southeast Asia, such as Thai Buddha images, Burmese lacquerware, Indonesian batik textiles, and Vietnamese ceramics, representing the region's artistic diversity and cultural influences.

Experiences and Recommendations

• The museum offers cultural workshops, demonstrations, and hands-on activities to teach visitors about traditional Asian crafts, calligraphy, tea ceremonies, and artistic skills.

• Thematic Exhibitions: The museum curates rotating displays on certain locations, artistic styles, historical periods, or cross-cultural themes, providing insights into Asia's artistic heritage and worldwide linkages.

• The museum offers multimedia presentations, audio guides, and digital tools for learning about Asian art and culture. These resources provide cultural context and interactive encounters.

• The museum's cafes, cultural events, and themed evenings promote leisure, socialization, and cultural exchange through live performances, film screenings, and culinary experiences inspired by Asian customs.

Outdoor Adventures on Corfu: Embracing Nature's Beauty

Corfu, with its breathtaking sceneries, blue oceans, and mountainous terrain, invites outdoor enthusiasts to discover its natural beauties and embark on fascinating experiences. Corfu's outdoor activities range from sun-kissed beaches to stunning hiking routes and challenging off-road experiences, catering to the spirit of every adventurer. In this guide, we'll take a look at three interesting outdoor excursions in Corfu: beaches and water activities, hiking routes, and Jeep safaris. We'll look at the experiences, activities, and adrenaline-pumping adventures that await visitors looking to immerse themselves in Corfu's natural splendor.

Beaches & Water Activities
Beach Paradises

1. Paleokastritsa Beach: Nestled amidst lush greenery and turquoise waters, Paleokastritsa Beach is a postcard-perfect paradise offering sunbathing, swimming, and snorkeling opportunities. Explore nearby caves by boat or kayak for a unique coastal adventure.

2. Glyfada Beach: Popular among beachgoers and water sports enthusiasts due to its golden sands and clean waters.

Try parasailing, jet skiing, or paddleboarding for a thrill on the waves.

3. Agios Georgios Beach: This long sandy beach with shallow seas is great for families and leisurely swims. For an unforgettable water adventure, rent a pedal boat or a stand-up paddleboard and explore the shoreline.

4. Kerasia Beach: A hidden cove with natural beauty, ideal for a relaxed day by the sea. Snorkel with colorful marine life or have a beach picnic surrounded by olive groves and crystal-clear waters.

Water Adventures

1. Scuba Diving: Explore Corfu's underwater world with scuba diving excursions that reveal vibrant reefs, marine life, and shipwrecks teeming with history and biodiversity. Dive centers in Paleokastritsa and Ipsos offer courses and guided dives for divers of all levels.

2. Windsurfing and Kitesurfing: The island's windy shores, particularly in Agios Gordios and Acharavi, are ideal for windsurfing and kitesurfing enthusiasts. Glide across the waves and harness the power of the wind for an exhilarating ride on the water.

3. Boat Tours and Cruises: Embark on boat tours and cruises that explore Corfu's coastline, hidden coves, and neighboring islands. From sunset cruises to day trips to Paxos and Antipaxos, there are plenty of nautical adventures to choose from.

4. Kayaking and Paddleboarding: Rent a kayak or paddleboard to explore Corfu's coast at your own pace, discovering secluded beaches, sea caves, and marine habitats along the way. Guided tours and equipment rentals are available in popular beach areas.

Hiking Trails

Nature Escapes

1. Corfu Trail: Spanning the length of the island, the Corfu Trail offers hikers a scenic journey through diverse landscapes, including olive groves, vineyards, coastal cliffs, and traditional villages. Choose from day hikes or multi-day treks to immerse in Corfu's natural beauty.

2. Mount Pantokrator: Conquer the highest peak in Corfu, Mount Pantokrator, on a challenging yet rewarding hike. Enjoy panoramic views of the Ionian Sea, neighboring islands, and lush valleys as you ascend to the summit.

3. Ropa Valley: Explore the scenic Ropa Valley, known for its biodiversity, wildlife, and rural charm.

Follow hiking trails that wind through forests, meadows, and agricultural terraces, encountering local flora and fauna along the way.

4. Angelokastro Trail: Walk in the footsteps of history on the Angelokastro Trail, leading to the ancient Byzantine fortress perched atop a rocky cliff.

Marvel at panoramic vistas, archaeological ruins, and medieval fortifications as you trek through rugged terrain.

Adventure Highlights

1. Canyoning and Gorge Exploration: Discover Corfu's hidden gems on canyoning adventures that navigate natural waterfalls, rock pools, and narrow gorges. Experienced guides lead thrilling expeditions in locations like Nymphes Gorge and Arkoudilas Canyon.

2. Exploring Coastal Paths: Follow coastal paths and seaside trails that showcase Corfu's coastal beauty, dramatic cliffs, and hidden beaches. Pack a picnic and venture along routes like the Corfu Trail's coastal sections for scenic hikes with ocean views.

3. Birdwatching and Nature Photography: Corfu's diverse ecosystems, including wetlands, forests, and coastal habitats, offer opportunities for birdwatching and nature photography. Spot migratory birds, rare species, and scenic landscapes in protected areas like Korission Lagoon and Pantokratoras Mountain.

4. Guided Nature Walks: Join guided nature walks and eco-tours led by local experts and naturalists who share insights into Corfu's flora, fauna, and environmental conservation efforts.

Learn about sustainable practices and the island's ecological diversity while exploring nature reserves and protected areas.

Jeep Safaris

Offroad Adventures

1. **North Corfu Jeep Safari:** Experience an exciting off-road adventure through the mountainous terrain, olive groves, and quaint towns of North Corfu. Explore the island's rural charm by following dirt paths, mountain hikes, and breathtaking vistas.

2. **Jeep Safari in South Corfu:** Explore the island's quiet beaches, scenic cliffs, and historical landmarks. Along the trip, you can stop at traditional tavernas, olive presses, and scenic locations.

3. **Mountain Explorer Safari:** Explore Corfu's mountainous interior, including secluded towns, old ruins, and natural wonders. Explore local culture, traditional crafts, and panoramic views from mountaintops.

4. **Sunset Safari Adventure:** Experience the magic of a sunset safari adventure that combines off-road exploration with sunset views from scenic locations. Capture unforgettable moments and enjoy a barbecue dinner under the stars for a memorable outdoor experience.

Adventure Highlights

1. Local Encounters: Jeep safaris provide an opportunity to interact with people and learn about their traditional lifestyles, farming practices, and cultural heritage. For truly authentic experiences, go to family-run tavernas, agrotourism destinations, and artisan workshops.
2. Jeep safaris provide panoramic views of Corfu's natural surroundings, including mountain ranges and seaside cliffs. Photograph stunning views, wildlife observations, and geological formations along the trip.
3. Jeep safaris conducted by skilled guides offer unique opportunities to explore ancient locations, historical landmarks, and hidden jewels. Discover Corfu's history, mythology, and archaeological treasures while exploring remote locations unreachable by conventional vehicles.
4. Adventure and Adrenaline: Experience the thrill of off-road driving, river crossings, and rugged trails on Jeep safaris designed for adventure seekers and nature enthusiasts. Enjoy the freedom of exploration and the excitement of outdoor discovery in Corfu's wild landscapes.

Cultural Experiences in Corfu: Embracing Tradition and Flavor

Corfu, a treasure mine of history, culture, and gastronomic delights, welcomes visitors to immerse themselves in its bustling cultural activities. Corfu's rich legacy is reflected in its colorful festivals, hands-on cooking workshops, and wine-tasting trips. In this book, we'll take you on a journey through three unforgettable cultural experiences in Corfu: festivals and events, cooking classes, and wine-tasting tours. We'll look at the cultural significance, cuisines, and immersive experiences that await travelers eager to uncover Corfu's cultural tapestry and culinary delights.

Festivals & Events

Colorful celebrations

1. Easter Celebrations: Experience the vibrant traditions of Easter in Corfu, known for its unique customs, religious processions, and cultural festivities. Witness the "Botides" ceremony, where clay pots are thrown from balconies, symbolizing the resurrection.

2. Corfu Carnival: Join the lively Corfu Carnival, a spectacle of music, dance, and costume parades that mark the pre-Lenten season with colorful floats, masked performers, and street parties. Enjoy the festive atmosphere and traditional "kantades" songs.

3. Saint Spyridon Feast: Celebrate the patron saint of Corfu, Saint Spyridon, during the feast day on December 12th, with religious processions, church services, and cultural events honoring the saint's miracles and legacy.

4. Summer Music Festivals: Attend summer music festivals and cultural events held in Corfu Town, featuring live performances, concerts, and theatrical productions showcasing local talent, international artists, and diverse musical genres.

Experiences and Recommendations

• **Cultural Immersion:** Immerse yourself in local traditions, folklore, and customs during festivals and events, interacting with locals, participating in rituals, and experiencing the island's festive spirit.
• **Photography Opportunities:** Capture colorful moments, costumes, and cultural performances during festivals and events, documenting the dynamic energy, creativity, and traditions of Corfu's cultural celebrations.
• **Culinary Delights:** Taste traditional dishes, sweets, and specialties prepared during festive occasions, such as Easter "tsoureki" bread, Carnival "fritters," and

Saint Spyridon's feast day treats, for a culinary journey through Corfu's festive cuisine.

• **Art and Craft Fairs:** Explore art exhibitions, craft fairs, and cultural markets organized during festivals and events, showcasing local artists, artisans, and traditional crafts, from pottery and textiles to jewelry and folk art.

Cooking Classes

Gastronomic Adventures

1. Local Cuisine: Learn the secrets of Corfiot cuisine in cooking classes led by expert chefs and local cooks, who share recipes, techniques, and ingredients for traditional dishes like "pastitsada," "bourdeto," and "sofrito."

2. Farm-to-Table Experience: Participate in farm-to-table cooking experiences that highlight Corfu's agricultural heritage, seasonal produce, and organic ingredients sourced from local farms, orchards, and markets.

3. Seafood Specialties: Discover the art of preparing fresh seafood dishes, including grilled octopus, stuffed squid, and seafood risotto, using locally caught fish and shellfish in hands-on cooking sessions by the sea.

4. Olive Oil and Vinegar: Explore the flavors of Corfu's olive oil and vinegar in cooking classes focused on Mediterranean recipes, dressings, and marinades that showcase the island's olive groves and vineyards.

Experiences and Recommendations

• **Hands-On Cooking:** Roll up your sleeves and participate in hands-on cooking classes, where you'll chop, sauté, and simmer traditional Corfiot dishes under the guidance of local chefs and culinary experts.
• **Market Visits:** Join culinary tours and market visits to local markets, fishing harbors, and artisanal shops to source fresh ingredients, spices, and specialty products for cooking classes and culinary experiences.
• **Wine Pairing Dinners:** Enjoy wine pairing dinners and gastronomic experiences that combine cooking classes with wine tastings, showcasing the harmony of flavors between Corfu's cuisine and local wines.
• **Cooking Competitions:** Test your culinary skills and creativity in cooking competitions or friendly cook-offs organized as part of cooking classes and culinary events, with prizes for the most delicious dishes.

Wine Tasting Tours

Vinicultural Explorations

1. Local Vineyards: Visit traditional vineyards and wineries in Corfu's countryside, where you can tour the cellars, learn about winemaking techniques, and sample a variety of local wines, including Robola, Moschofilero, and Verdea.

2. Wine Trails: Follow wine trails and tasting routes that showcase Corfu's wine regions, terroirs, and grape varietals, offering scenic views, historical insights, and tastings of red, white, and rosé wines.

3. Gastronomic Pairings: Experience wine-tasting tours paired with gastronomic delights, such as cheese platters, olive oil tastings, and traditional snacks that complement the flavors and aromas of Corfu's wines.

4. Wine Festivals: Attend wine festivals, tastings, and wine-themed events held in Corfu, featuring local winemakers, sommeliers, and wine enthusiasts who share their knowledge, passion, and appreciation for the island's wines.

Experiences and Recommendations

- **Guided Wine Tours**: Join guided wine tours and tastings led by sommeliers, wine experts, and local vintners who provide insights into Corfu's wine heritage, vineyard practices, and wine culture.
- **Vineyard Visits**: Explore picturesque vineyards, historic estates, and family-run wineries during wine-tasting tours, where you can stroll among the vines, sample wines

straight from the barrel, and learn about grape varieties.

- **Wine Education**: Attend wine education sessions, workshops, and masterclasses offered as part of wine-tasting tours, covering topics such as wine pairing, tasting techniques, and the art of wine appreciation.
- **Wine and Dine Experiences**: Indulge in wine and dine experiences that combine wine tasting with gourmet meals, farm-to-table dinners, or sunset picnics in scenic vineyard settings, creating memorable gastronomic moments.

Conclusion

Corfu's cultural experiences, including festivals and events, cooking classes, and wine-tasting tours, offer a tapestry of traditions, flavors, and sensory delights for travelers seeking to immerse themselves in the island's rich heritage and gastronomic heritage. Whether celebrating colorful festivals, mastering Corfiot cuisine, or savoring local wines, visitors can engage in immersive experiences that showcase Corfu's vibrant culture, culinary diversity, and hospitality. By embracing cultural activities, travelers can deepen their connection to Corfu's traditions, flavors, and community spirit, creating lasting memories and enriching their cultural exploration of the island.

CHAPTER FOUR
Dining and Culinary Experiences in Corfu: A Gastronomic Journey

Corfu, with its rich culinary heritage and Mediterranean flavors, provides a gourmet journey unlike any other. From traditional Greek cuisine to seafood specialties and the well-known Corfiot olive oil, the island's dining scene celebrates fresh ingredients, authentic flavors, and centuries-old traditions. In this guide, we'll look at the various gastronomic experiences in Corfu, highlighting local cuisine and delicacies that tickle the taste senses while reflecting the island's cultural richness.

Traditional Greek dishes

The flavors of Greece

1. Moussaka is a popular Greek meal that combines eggplant, minced meat (usually lamb or beef), tomatoes, onions, and béchamel sauce, cooked to perfection. It's a rich and warming recipe that highlights a variety of Mediterranean seasonings

2. Souvlaki: Grilled skewers of marinated meat, typically pork or chicken, souvlaki is a popular street food in Greece.

Served with pita bread, tzatziki sauce, and fresh vegetables, it's a flavorful and satisfying dish enjoyed by locals and visitors alike.

3. Dolmades: Stuffed grape leaves filled with a mixture of rice, herbs, and sometimes minced meat, dolmades are a classic appetizer or meze in Greek cuisine. Served with lemon wedges and olive oil, they offer a burst of flavors in every bite.

4. Spanakopita: A savory pie made with layers of phyllo pastry, spinach, feta cheese, onions, and herbs, spanakopita is a delicious vegetarian dish that highlights the freshness of Greek ingredients and the delicate crunch of phyllo.

Experiences and Recommendations

• Taverna Dining: Visit local tavernas and traditional restaurants in Corfu Town, villages, and coastal areas to savor authentic Greek dishes prepared with locally sourced ingredients, accompanied by local wines or ouzo.

• Cooking Workshops: Participate in cooking workshops and culinary experiences where you can learn to prepare traditional Greek dishes under the guidance of skilled chefs, using fresh herbs, spices, and olive oil.

• Food Markets: Explore food markets, farmers' markets, and specialty shops in Corfu to discover regional products, artisanal cheeses, olives, honey, and other ingredients used in Greek cuisine, ideal for culinary enthusiasts and foodies.

• Gastronomic Tours: Join gastronomic tours and tasting experiences that introduce you to the flavors of Corfu's traditional dishes, mezes, desserts, and beverages, offering insights into the island's culinary traditions and heritage.

Seafood Delicacies

Fresh from the Sea

1. Grilled Octopus: A Mediterranean delicacy, grilled octopus is tenderized and then charred on the grill, served with olive oil, lemon, and herbs. It's a flavorful and succulent seafood dish that pairs well with Greek salads or ouzo.

2. Seafood Risotto: Creamy risotto infused with the flavors of fresh seafood, including shrimp, mussels, and calamari, seafood risotto is a luxurious dish that showcases the bounty of the Ionian Sea and the skill of Corfiot chefs.

3. Stuffed Squid: Tender squid tubes stuffed with a mixture of breadcrumbs, herbs, and seafood, then grilled or baked to perfection, stuffed squid is a flavorful and elegant seafood dish often served with lemon and parsley.

4. Fisherman's Soup: A hearty and aromatic soup made with a variety of fresh fish, shellfish, vegetables, and herbs, fisherman's soup is a beloved dish in coastal regions of Corfu, showcasing the island's maritime culinary traditions.

Experiences and Recommendations

• Seafood Restaurants: Dine at seafood restaurants and tavernas along the coast of Corfu, where you can enjoy fresh catch-of-the-day dishes, seafood platters, and grilled specialties overlooking the sea.

• Seafood Markets: Visit local seafood markets, fishing harbors, and seaside villages to witness the daily catch, interact with fishermen, and purchase fresh seafood for cooking or seafood barbecues by the beach.

• Fish Feasts: Attend fish festivals, seafood feasts, and culinary events celebrating Corfu's maritime heritage, where you can taste a variety of seafood dishes, grilled fish, seafood paellas, and seafood stews.

• Cooking with Fish: Enroll in cooking classes or workshops focused on seafood preparation and fish dishes, where you can learn techniques for cleaning, filleting, and cooking fish and shellfish in traditional Corfiot styles.

Olive Oil Tastings

Liquid Gold of Corfu

1. Extra Virgin Olive Oil: Corfu is renowned for its high-quality extra virgin olive oil, produced from local olive varieties such as Koroneiki and Lianolia. The olive oil is prized for its fruity flavors, peppery notes, and health benefits.

2. Olive Oil Dips: Enjoy olive oil tastings with bread or crusty ciabatta, dipping into pure olive oil infused with herbs, garlic, or chili flakes for a flavorful and aromatic experience that showcases the versatility of olive oil.

3. Olive Oil Varietals: Explore the nuances of different olive oil varietals and blends during olive oil tastings, learning about production methods, harvesting techniques, and the art of olive oil extraction.

4. Cooking with Olive Oil: Discover the use of olive oil in Corfiot cuisine through cooking classes or culinary experiences that highlight olive oil-based dishes, dressings, marinades, and desserts.

Experiences and Recommendations

• Olive Oil Tours: Take guided tours of olive groves, olive oil mills, and family-owned estates in Corfu to learn about olive cultivation, harvesting, pressing, and the production of extra virgin olive oil.

• Tasting Workshops: Attend olive oil tasting workshops and seminars led by olive oil experts and producers who educate participants on olive oil tasting techniques, flavor profiles, and quality standards.

• Olive Oil Pairings: Explore the art of olive oil pairings with food, wine, and cheese, discovering how different olive oil varietals enhance flavors and complement dishes in Corfu's culinary traditions.

• Olive Oil Festivals: Celebrate the olive harvest season at olive oil festivals, tastings, and cultural events held in Corfu, where you can sample fresh olive oil, enjoy olive-related activities, and learn about the significance of olives in Greek culture.

Exploring Popular Restaurants and Cafes

Corfu's dining landscape is a blend of traditional flavors, seafront ambiance, and cozy cafes, offering a diverse culinary experience that delights locals and visitors alike. From seafood delights by the sea to tavernas serving authentic Greek dishes and charming cafes for coffee and pastries, Corfu's dining scene caters to every palate and preference. In this guide, we'll explore some of the island's popular restaurants and cafes, showcasing their unique offerings, picturesque settings, and flavorful delights.

Seafront Dining

Coastal Gastronomy

1. The Wave: Located along Corfu's stunning coastline, The Wave offers a seafront dining experience with panoramic views of the Ionian Sea. The restaurant specializes in fresh seafood dishes, grilled octopus, and seafood risotto, paired with local wines and cocktails.

2. Seaside Taverna: Nestled by the beach in a picturesque cove, Seaside Taverna is known for its Mediterranean cuisine, seafood platters, and sunset views. Dine al fresco and savor grilled fish, stuffed squid, and Greek mezes while listening to the sound of waves.

3. Ocean Breeze Restaurant: Offering a breezy atmosphere and ocean vistas, Ocean Breeze Restaurant is a favorite for seafood lovers and sunset diners.

Enjoy lobster pasta, grilled shrimp, and fresh catch of the day, complemented by local wines and sea breezes.

4. Beachfront Grill: For a casual beachside dining experience, Beachfront Grill serves up grilled specialties, seafood BBQs, and refreshing cocktails right on the sand. Relax under umbrellas, savoring grilled octopus skewers and Greek salads with a sea view.

Experiences and Recommendations

• Romantic Dinners: Plan romantic dinners by the sea at seafront restaurants, choosing candlelit tables, sunset views, and fresh seafood specialties for unforgettable dining experiences.

• Family Gatherings: Organize family gatherings and celebrations at seafront venues that offer spacious outdoor seating, kids' menus, and a relaxed atmosphere for all generations to enjoy.

• Special Occasions: Celebrate special occasions such as birthdays, anniversaries, and engagements with customized menus, private dining areas, and personalized service at seafront establishments.

• Beachside Events: Attend beachside events, live music performances, and themed parties hosted by seafront restaurants, combining dining with entertainment and beachside fun.

Tavernas with Authentic Flavors

Rustic Charm and Traditional Dishes

1. Korfiotiko Taverna: Embracing Corfu's culinary heritage, Korfiotiko Taverna offers a rustic ambiance and authentic flavors. Sample traditional dishes like moussaka, souvlaki, and stuffed peppers, accompanied by local wines and Greek music.

2. Ouzeri O Nikos: A cozy ouzeri in the heart of Corfu Town, Ouzeri O Nikos is renowned for its mezes, ouzo pairings, and lively atmosphere. Try grilled sardines, fava bean dip, and fried calamari while soaking in the taverna's charm.

3. Traditional Kafeneio: Step into a traditional kafeneio-turned-taverna for a taste of village life and hearty dishes. Enjoy slow-cooked lamb, oven-baked feta, and homemade bread, accompanied by local tsipouro or raki.

4. Taverna Stavros: Family-owned and steeped in tradition, Taverna Stavros serves up Corfiot classics and grilled specialties in a friendly setting. Feast on grilled meats, Greek salads, and spanakopita, paired with house wine or ouzo.

Experiences and Recommendations

• Local Ingredients: Taste the flavors of Corfu's countryside and coastline at tavernas using locally sourced ingredients, from olive oil and herbs to cheese, honey, and fresh produce.

• Live Music Nights: Enjoy live music nights at tavernas featuring traditional Greek music, bouzouki players, and dance performances, adding to the lively ambiance and cultural experience.

• Meze Feasts: Indulge in meze feasts at tavernas, ordering a variety of small plates to share with friends and family, accompanied by ouzo, raki, or local wines for a convivial dining experience.

• Cooking Demonstrations: Attend cooking demonstrations and workshops at tavernas that showcase traditional recipes, cooking techniques, and the art of Corfiot cuisine, offering insights into local culinary traditions.

Cafes for Coffee and Pastries

Coffee Culture and Sweet Treats

1. Café Eptanisa: A cozy café overlooking Corfu's old town, Café Eptanisa is a favorite spot for coffee lovers and pastry enthusiasts. Sip freshly brewed coffee,

cappuccino, or frappe, paired with homemade pastries and desserts.

2. Bakery & Coffee House: Combining a bakery and coffee house, this charming café offers artisanal bread, pastries, and cakes alongside espresso drinks, lattes, and herbal teas. Relax with a book or chat with friends over a slice of baklava.

3. Patisserie Paradiso: Step into a world of sweet delights at Patisserie Paradiso, where French-inspired pastries, macarons, and éclairs tempt the senses. Pair your pastry with a specialty coffee or hot chocolate for a decadent treat.

4. Café Bougatsa: Specializing in bougatsa, a traditional Greek pastry filled with custard or cheese, Café Bougatsa is a must-visit for pastry aficionados. Enjoy a warm slice of bougatsa with a side of Greek coffee or frappe.

Experiences and Recommendations

• Coffee Rituals: Experience Greek coffee rituals at cafes, from strong Greek coffee served in traditional briki pots to freddo espresso and freddo cappuccino, perfect for hot summer days.

• Pastry Tastings: Explore pastry tastings and dessert samplers at cafes, sampling a variety of Greek sweets, baklava, kataifi, galaktoboureko, and loukoumades, paired with herbal teas or iced beverages.

• Artisanal Bakeries: Visit artisanal bakeries and patisseries to discover handcrafted bread, cakes, and pastries made with local ingredients and traditional techniques, ideal for breakfast, snacks, or sweet indulgences.

• Café Culture: Immerse yourself in café culture, spending leisurely hours at cafes with outdoor seating, people-watching, reading, or simply enjoying the laid-back atmosphere and aromas of freshly brewed coffee.

Conclusion

Corfu's popular restaurants and cafes offer a diverse range of dining experiences, from seafront elegance and taverna charm to cozy cafes for coffee and pastries. Whether indulging in seafood delights by the sea, savoring authentic Greek dishes at tavernas, or enjoying coffee rituals and sweet treats at cafes, visitors can immerse themselves in Corfu's culinary delights, scenic settings, and cultural ambiance. By exploring the island's dining and culinary scene, travelers can taste the flavors of Corfu, connect with local traditions, and create memorable gastronomic experiences that reflect the essence of the island's hospitality and culinary heritage.

Shopping and Souvenirs in Corfu: Exploring Vibrant Shopping Districts

Corfu's commercial areas offer a beautiful blend of traditional crafts, local items, and one-of-a-kind souvenirs, making it a shopping and souvenir paradise. From quaint pedestrian walkways to bustling markets, the island's shopping sector offers tourists the opportunity to discover artisan products, culinary snacks, stylish bargains, and cultural treasures. In this guide, we'll look at three bustling shopping districts in Corfu: Liston Street, Corfu Town Market, and Kerkyraikos Market, highlighting their offerings, atmosphere, and must-see businesses.

Liston Saint

Elegance and History

1. Liston Arcade: Named after the French "Liston" style of architecture, this lovely arcade in Corfu Town features elegant cafés, stores, and neoclassical buildings. Stroll down the marble pavement, admiring the Venetian influence and local craftsmanship.

2. Boutique Shops: Explore boutique shops on Liston Street offering designer clothing, jewelry, and accessories inspired by Corfu's culture and

Mediterranean style. Discover unique pieces crafted by local artisans and designers.

3. Art Galleries: Discover works by Greek and foreign artists, including paintings, sculptures, ceramics, and contemporary art. Liston Street's art scene reflects Corfu's cultural legacy and creative energy.

4. Relax in traditional cafés on Liston Street, sipping coffee, frappes, or cocktails with views of Spianada Square, cricket grounds, and old architecture. It's an ideal location for people-watching and taking in the atmosphere.

Experiences and Recommendations

• Local Crafts: Shop on Liston Street for handmade jewelry, leather products, textiles, and ceramics that reflect Corfu's artistic traditions.

• Café Culture: Experience café culture on Liston Street by sampling traditional Greek coffee, pastries like bougatsa or baklava, and local delicacies while admiring the architecture and lively atmosphere.

• Evening Strolls: Take evening strolls along Liston Street when the lights illuminate the arcade, creating a magical ambiance for shopping, dining, and leisurely walks under the starry sky.

• Photography Opportunities: Capture the beauty of Liston Street with its iconic arcades, colorful façades, and historical landmarks, making it a picturesque setting for photography enthusiasts.

Corfu Town Market

Local Flavors and Delights

1. Fresh Produce Stalls: Corfu Town Market, also known as Agora, is a bustling hub of activity offering fresh fruits, vegetables, herbs, and local produce sourced from nearby farms and gardens. Experience the vibrant colors and aromas of the market.

2. Fish and Seafood Market: Explore the fish and seafood market section, where fishermen display their daily catch of fish, shellfish, and seafood specialties. It's a paradise for seafood lovers looking to cook or taste fresh marine delicacies.

3. Local Delicacies: Sample local delicacies such as olives, cheeses, honey, pastries, and cured meats at specialty food stalls in Corfu Town Market. Taste traditional flavors and discover gourmet treats made with love and expertise.

4. Artisanal Crafts: Browse through artisanal crafts and handmade goods at market stalls, including pottery,

textiles, souvenirs, and decorative items that reflect Corfu's cultural heritage and artisanal craftsmanship.

Experiences and Recommendations

• Market Day Excursions: Plan visits to Corfu Town Market on market days, usually bustling on weekday mornings, to experience the lively atmosphere, interact with vendors, and purchase fresh ingredients and local products.

• Cooking Workshops: Combine a visit to Corfu Town Market with cooking workshops or culinary experiences, where you can learn to prepare Greek dishes using market-fresh ingredients under the guidance of local chefs.

• Tasting Tours: Join food tasting tours and gastronomic experiences that include stops at Corfu Town Market, sampling a variety of flavors, specialties, and gourmet treats while learning about the island's culinary traditions.

• Gift Shopping: Shop for unique gifts and souvenirs at Corfu Town Market, selecting from a range of artisanal crafts, local products, and food items that make perfect gifts for friends and family back home.

Kerkyraikos Market

Hidden Gems and Antiques

1. Antique Alley: Kerkyraikos Market, located in the heart of Corfu Town, is a treasure trove of antique shops, vintage finds, and collectibles. Explore Antique Alley for unique artifacts, retro items, and historical memorabilia.

2. Vintage Fashion: Discover vintage fashion boutiques and clothing stores in Kerkyraikos Market, offering retro apparel, accessories, and one-of-a-kind pieces that blend old-world charm with modern style.

3. Artisan Workshops: Visit artisan workshops and studios in Kerkyraikos Market, where local craftsmen create handmade jewelry, ceramics, leather goods, and artistic creations using traditional techniques.

4. Curio Shops: Browse curio shops and eclectic stores for curious finds, quirky souvenirs, and whimsical items that add a touch of personality to your home or serve as memorable gifts for collectors and enthusiasts.

Experiences and Recommendations

• Antique Hunting: Embark on a treasure hunt in Kerkyraikos Market, exploring antique shops, flea markets, and vintage stores for rare finds, historical artifacts, and unique pieces that tell stories of the past.

• Collectibles Fair: Attend collectibles fairs, antique markets, and vintage expos held in Kerkyraikos Market, where you can buy, sell, or trade antiques, retro items, and memorabilia with fellow enthusiasts and dealers.

• Artistic Discoveries: Dive into the artistic scene of Kerkyraikos Market by visiting art galleries, studios, and exhibitions featuring contemporary artworks, sculptures, paintings, and mixed-media creations by local artists.

• Cultural Immersion: Immerse yourself in the cultural heritage of Corfu at Kerkyraikos Market, discovering traditions, craftsmanship, and storytelling through antique objects, handicrafts, and cultural artifacts.

Unique Souvenirs in Corfu: Discovering Local Crafts and Treasures

Corfu provides a gourmet trip unlike any other. From traditional Greek cuisine to seafood specialties and the well-known Corfiot olive oil, the island's dining scene celebrates fresh ingredients, authentic flavors, and centuries-old traditions.

In this guide, we'll look at the various gastronomic experiences in Corfu, highlighting local cuisine and delicacies that tickle the taste senses while reflecting the island's cultural richness.

Traditional Greek dishes

The flavors of Greece

1. Moussaka is a popular Greek meal that combines eggplant, minced meat (usually lamb or beef), tomatoes, onions, and béchamel sauce, cooked to perfection. It's a rich and warming recipe that highlights a variety of Mediterranean seasonings.

2. Souvlaki: Grilled skewers of marinated meat, typically pork or chicken, souvlaki is a popular street food in Greece. Served with pita bread, tzatziki sauce, and fresh vegetables, it's a flavorful and satisfying dish enjoyed by locals and visitors alike.

3. Dolmades: Stuffed grape leaves filled with a mixture of rice, herbs, and sometimes minced meat, dolmades are a classic appetizer or meze in Greek cuisine. Served with lemon wedges and olive oil, they offer a burst of flavors in every bite.

4. Spanakopita: A savory pie made with layers of phyllo pastry, spinach, feta cheese, onions, and herbs, spanakopita is a delicious vegetarian dish that

highlights the freshness of Greek ingredients and the delicate crunch of phyllo.

Experiences and Recommendations

- **Taverna Dining**: Visit local tavernas and traditional restaurants in Corfu Town, villages, and coastal areas to savor authentic Greek dishes prepared with locally sourced ingredients, accompanied by local wines or ouzo.
- **Cooking Workshops**: Participate in cooking workshops and culinary experiences where you can learn to prepare traditional Greek dishes under the guidance of skilled chefs, using fresh herbs, spices, and olive oil.
- **Food Markets**: Explore food markets, farmers' markets, and specialty shops in Corfu to discover regional products, artisanal cheeses, olives, honey, and other ingredients used in Greek cuisine, ideal for culinary enthusiasts and foodies.
- **Gastronomic Tours**: Join gastronomic tours and tasting experiences that introduce you to the flavors of Corfu's traditional dishes, mezes, desserts, and beverages, offering insights into the island's culinary traditions and heritage.

Seafood Delicacies

Fresh from the Sea

1. **Grilled Octopus**: A Mediterranean delicacy, grilled octopus is tenderized and then charred on the grill, served with olive oil, lemon, and herbs. It's a flavorful and succulent seafood dish that pairs well with Greek salads or ouzo.
2. **Seafood Risotto**: Creamy risotto infused with the flavors of fresh seafood, including shrimp, mussels, and calamari, seafood risotto is a luxurious dish that showcases the bounty of the Ionian Sea and the skill of Corfiot chefs.
3. **Stuffed Squid**: Tender squid tubes stuffed with a mixture of breadcrumbs, herbs, and seafood, then grilled or baked to perfection, stuffed squid is a flavorful and elegant seafood dish often served with lemon and parsley.
4. **Fisherman's Soup**: A hearty and aromatic soup made with a variety of fresh fish, shellfish, vegetables, and herbs, fisherman's soup is a beloved dish in coastal regions of Corfu, showcasing the island's maritime culinary traditions.

Experiences and Recommendations

- **Seafood Restaurants**: Dine at seafood restaurants and tavernas along the coast of

Corfu, where you can enjoy fresh catch-of-the-day dishes, seafood platters, and grilled specialties overlooking the sea.

- **Seafood Markets**: Visit local seafood markets, fishing harbors, and seaside villages to witness the daily catch, interact with fishermen, and purchase fresh seafood for cooking or seafood barbecues by the beach.
- **Fish Feasts**: Attend fish festivals, seafood feasts, and culinary events celebrating Corfu's maritime heritage, where you can taste a variety of seafood dishes, grilled fish, seafood paellas, and seafood stews.
- **Cooking with Fish**: Enroll in cooking classes or workshops focused on seafood preparation and fish dishes, where you can learn techniques for cleaning, filleting, and cooking fish and shellfish in traditional Corfiot styles.

Olive Oil Tasting
Liquid Gold of Corfu

1. **Extra Virgin Olive Oil**: Corfu is renowned for its high-quality extra virgin olive oil, produced from local olive varieties such as Koroneiki and Lianolia. The olive oil is prized for its fruity flavors, peppery notes, and health benefits.

2. **Olive Oil Dips**: Enjoy olive oil tastings with bread or crusty ciabatta, dipping into pure olive

oil infused with herbs, garlic, or chili flakes for a flavorful and aromatic experience that showcases the versatility of olive oil.

3. **Olive Oil Varietals**: Explore the nuances of different olive oil varietals and blends during olive oil tastings, learning about production methods, harvesting techniques, and the art of olive oil extraction.

4. **Cooking with Olive Oil**: Discover the use of olive oil in Corfiot cuisine through cooking classes or culinary experiences that highlight olive oil-based dishes, dressings, marinades, and desserts.

Experiences and Recommendations

- **Olive Oil Tours**: Take guided tours of olive groves, olive oil mills, and family-owned estates in Corfu to learn about olive cultivation, harvesting, pressing, and the production of extra virgin olive oil.

- **Tasting Workshops**: Attend olive oil tasting workshops and seminars led by olive oil experts and producers who educate participants on olive oil tasting techniques, flavor profiles, and quality standards.

- **Olive Oil Pairings**: Explore the art of olive oil pairings with food, wine, and cheese, discovering how different olive oil varietals enhance flavors and complement dishes in Corfu's culinary traditions.

- **Olive Oil Festivals**: Celebrate the olive harvest season at olive oil festivals, tastings, and cultural events held in Corfu, where you can sample fresh olive oil, enjoy olive-related activities, and learn about the significance of olives in Greek culture.

Conclusion

Corfu's dining and culinary experiences, from traditional Greek dishes and seafood delicacies to olive oil tastings, offer a gastronomic journey that celebrates the island's flavors, traditions, and natural bounty. Whether indulging in moussaka and grilled octopus, tasting extra virgin olive oil, or exploring seafood markets, visitors can immerse themselves in Corfu's culinary heritage, savoring authentic flavors and creating memorable gastronomic experiences. By embracing dining experiences, culinary tours, and tastings, travelers can discover the essence of Corfu's cuisine, hospitality, and cultural richness, forging connections through food and shared culinary traditions.

Dining and Culinary Experiences in Corfu: Exploring Popular Restaurants and Cafes

Corfu's dining scene combines traditional flavors, coastal ambiance, and small cafes, providing a diversified culinary experience that please both locals and visitors. Corfu's eating scene has something for everyone, from seafood delights by the sea to tavernas serving authentic Greek cuisine and quaint cafes for coffee and pastries. In this trip, we'll visit some of the island's most popular restaurants and cafes, highlighting their distinct offerings, stunning surroundings, and delectable cuisine.

Seafront Dining

Coastal gastronomy

1. The Wave, located on Corfu's magnificent coastline, provides a beachside dining experience with panoramic views of the Ionian Sea. The restaurant specializes in fresh seafood dishes, such as grilled octopus and seafood risotto, which are served with local wines and beverages.

2. Seaside Taverna: Nestled by the beach in a picturesque cove, Seaside Taverna is known for its

Mediterranean cuisine, seafood platters, and sunset views.

Dine al fresco and savor grilled fish, stuffed squid, and Greek mezes while listening to the sound of waves.

3. Ocean Breeze Restaurant: Offering a breezy atmosphere and ocean vistas, Ocean Breeze Restaurant is a favorite for seafood lovers and sunset diners. Enjoy lobster pasta, grilled shrimp, and fresh catch of the day, complemented by local wines and sea breezes.

4. Beachfront Grill: For a casual beachside dining experience, Beachfront Grill serves up grilled specialties, seafood BBQs, and refreshing cocktails right on the sand. Relax under umbrellas, savoring grilled octopus skewers and Greek salads with a sea view.

Experiences and Recommendations

• Romantic Dinners: Plan romantic dinners by the sea at seafront restaurants, choosing candlelit tables, sunset views, and fresh seafood specialties for unforgettable dining experiences.

• Family Gatherings: Organize family gatherings and celebrations at seafront venues that offer spacious outdoor seating, kids' menus, and a relaxed atmosphere for all generations to enjoy.

• Special Occasions: Celebrate special occasions such as birthdays, anniversaries, and engagements with customized menus, private dining areas, and personalized service at seafront establishments.

• Beachside Events: Attend beachside events, live music performances, and themed parties hosted by seafront restaurants, combining dining with entertainment and beachside fun.

Tavernas with Authentic Flavors

Rustic Charm and Traditional Dishes

1. Korfiotiko Taverna: Embracing Corfu's culinary heritage, Korfiotiko Taverna offers a rustic ambiance and authentic flavors. Sample traditional dishes like moussaka, souvlaki, and stuffed peppers, accompanied by local wines and Greek music.

2. Ouzeri O Nikos: A cozy ouzeri in the heart of Corfu Town, Ouzeri O Nikos is renowned for its mezes, ouzo pairings, and lively atmosphere. Try grilled sardines, fava bean dip, and fried calamari while soaking in the taverna's charm.

3. Traditional Kafeneio: Step into a traditional kafeneio-turned-taverna for a taste of village life and hearty dishes.

Enjoy slow-cooked lamb, oven-baked feta, and homemade bread, accompanied by local tsipouro or raki.

4. Taverna Stavros: Family-owned and steeped in tradition, Taverna Stavros serves up Corfiot classics and grilled specialties in a friendly setting. Feast on grilled meats, Greek salads, and spanakopita, paired with house wine or ouzo.

Experiences and Recommendations

• Local Ingredients: Taste the flavors of Corfu's countryside and coastline at tavernas using locally sourced ingredients, from olive oil and herbs to cheese, honey, and fresh produce.

• Live Music Nights: Enjoy live music nights at tavernas featuring traditional Greek music, bouzouki players, and dance performances, adding to the lively ambiance and cultural experience.

• Meze Feasts: Indulge in meze feasts at tavernas, ordering a variety of small plates to share with friends and family, accompanied by ouzo, raki, or local wines for a convivial dining experience.

• Cooking Demonstrations: Attend cooking demonstrations and workshops at tavernas that showcase traditional recipes, cooking techniques, and the art of Corfiot cuisine, offering insights into local culinary traditions.

Cafes for Coffee and Pastries

Coffee Culture and Sweet Treats

1. Café Eptanisa: A cozy café overlooking Corfu's old town, Café Eptanisa is a favorite spot for coffee lovers and pastry enthusiasts. Sip freshly brewed coffee, cappuccino, or frappe, paired with homemade pastries and desserts.

2. Bakery & Coffee House: Combining a bakery and coffee house, this charming café offers artisanal bread, pastries, and cakes alongside espresso drinks, lattes, and herbal teas. Relax with a book or chat with friends over a slice of baklava.

3. Patisserie Paradiso: Step into a world of sweet delights at Patisserie Paradiso, where French-inspired pastries, macarons, and éclairs tempt the senses. Pair your pastry with a specialty coffee or hot chocolate for a decadent treat.

4. Café Bougatsa: Specializing in bougatsa, a traditional Greek pastry filled with custard or cheese, Café Bougatsa is a must-visit for pastry aficionados. Enjoy a warm slice of bougatsa with a side of Greek coffee or frappe.

Experiences and Recommendations

• Coffee Rituals: Experience Greek coffee rituals at cafes, from strong Greek coffee served in traditional briki pots to freddo espresso and freddo cappuccino, perfect for hot summer days.

• Pastry Tastings: Explore pastry tastings and dessert samplers at cafes, sampling a variety of Greek sweets, baklava, kataifi, galaktoboureko, and loukoumades, paired with herbal teas or iced beverages.

• Artisanal Bakeries: Visit artisanal bakeries and patisseries to discover handcrafted bread, cakes, and pastries made with local ingredients and traditional techniques, ideal for breakfast, snacks, or sweet indulgences.

• Café Culture: Immerse yourself in café culture, spending leisurely hours at cafes with outdoor seating, people-watching, reading, or simply enjoying the laid-back atmosphere and aromas of freshly brewed coffee.

Shopping And Souvenirs

Unique Souvenirs in Corfu: Discovering Local Crafts and Treasures

Corfu, with its unique cultural past and artistic traditions, provides a treasure trove of one-of-a-kind souvenirs that encapsulate the island's beauty, workmanship, and Mediterranean charm.

From handcrafted artworks and olive products to exquisite jewelry inspired by Corfu's natural surroundings, shopping for souvenirs becomes an immersive experience in discovering the island's cultural diversity. In this guide, we will look at three types of unique souvenirs in Corfu: local crafts and artwork, olive products, and handcrafted jewelry, highlighting their skill, significance, and where to get them.

Local Crafts and Artworks

Artistic Expression and Heritage

1. pottery and Ceramics: Corfu's ceramic traditions span generations, with talented artists creating stunning vases, plates, and ornamental pieces. Each item shows the island's artistic tradition and Mediterranean influence.

2. Explore Corfu's art galleries and studios to see local artists' paintings, prints, and mixed-media works. Landscapes, seascapes, historic buildings, and cultural motifs that depict the beauty of the island are common themes.

3. Textiles and needlework: Explore Corfu's intricately crafted textiles and needlework, including traditional patterns, themes, and brilliant hues that reflect the island's cultural tapestry.

4. Woodcarvings and Sculptures: From olive wood carvings to marble sculptures, Corfu boasts a tradition of skilled artisans creating intricate works of art. Look for figurines, statues, and decorative items that showcase the island's natural beauty and craftsmanship.

Where to Find:

• Old Town Artisan Shops: Wander through the narrow streets of Corfu's Old Town, where artisan shops and galleries display a wide range of local crafts, artworks, and handmade treasures.

• Craft Markets and Festivals: Visit craft markets and cultural festivals held in Corfu, such as the Easter Fair and Summer Arts Festival, where local artisans showcase their creations and offer unique souvenirs.

• Artisan Workshops: Take a tour of artisan workshops and studios to witness the creative process firsthand and purchase directly from craftsmen specializing in pottery, textiles, woodworking, and more.

• Souvenir Shops: Explore souvenir shops throughout Corfu, especially in tourist areas and historic sites, where you can find a curated selection of local crafts, artwork, and souvenirs to take home.

Olive Products

Essence of the Mediterranean

1. Extra Virgin Olive Oil: Corfu is renowned for its high-quality olive oil, often referred to as "liquid gold." Purchase bottles of extra virgin olive oil produced from local olive groves, known for their rich flavor and health benefits.

2. Olive Wood Crafts: Discover unique olive wood products such as cutting boards, utensils, and decorative items crafted from the wood of Corfu's olive trees. The natural beauty and durability of olive wood make these souvenirs both practical and aesthetic.

3. Olive Oil Skincare: Pamper yourself with olive oil skincare products, including soaps, creams, and lotions made from pure olive oil. These natural

products nourish the skin and showcase the benefits of olive oil in beauty rituals.

4.   Olive-themed Gifts: Explore a range of olive-themed gifts and souvenirs, from olive-shaped trinkets and accessories to olive-themed kitchenware and home decor items that celebrate the Mediterranean symbol of peace and prosperity.

Where to Find:

• Olive Groves and Mills: Visit olive groves and olive oil mills in Corfu's countryside, where you can purchase freshly pressed olive oil, olive wood products, and olive-themed gifts directly from producers.

• Specialty Shops: Explore specialty shops and boutiques in Corfu Town and coastal villages that specialize in olive products, offering a wide range of olive oil varieties, skincare items, and unique souvenirs.

• Farmers' Markets: Shop at farmers' markets and local markets in Corfu, where you'll find stalls selling olive oil, olive wood crafts, and olive-based products alongside fresh produce and culinary delights.

• Olive Oil Tours: Take guided olive oil tours that include tastings, workshops, and visits to olive groves and mills, providing insights into the olive oil production process and opportunities to purchase authentic products.

Handmade Jewelry

Elegance and Craftsmanship

1. Silver Jewelry: Corfu is known for its exquisite silver jewelry, including rings, bracelets, necklaces, and earrings crafted by skilled silversmiths. Look for intricate designs inspired by nature, mythology, and traditional motifs.

2. Natural Gemstones: Discover jewelry adorned with natural gemstones such as turquoise, amethyst, and coral, sourced from the Mediterranean region and crafted into stunning pieces that reflect Corfu's coastal beauty.

3. Olive Leaf Designs: Embrace the symbolism of the olive tree with jewelry featuring olive leaf motifs, symbolic of peace, prosperity, and the Mediterranean heritage. Olive leaf earrings, pendants, and bracelets make meaningful gifts.

4. Custom Creations: Seek out jewelry stores and workshops offering custom-made pieces,

where you can collaborate with artisans to design personalized jewelry incorporating your preferences, initials, or meaningful symbols.

Where to Find:

• Jewelry Districts: Explore jewelry districts and shopping areas in Corfu Town, such as Kapodistriou Street and Guilford Street, where you'll find a variety of jewelry stores, boutiques, and workshops.

• Artisan Boutiques: Visit artisan boutiques and designer studios specializing in handmade jewelry, where you can browse unique collections, discuss custom designs, and purchase one-of-a-kind pieces.

• Craft Fairs and Exhibitions: Attend craft fairs, jewelry exhibitions, and cultural events held in Corfu, where local jewelers showcase their creations, offer demonstrations, and interact with visitors interested in unique jewelry.

• Online Platforms: Explore online platforms and websites featuring Corfu's jewelry designers and artisans, offering a convenient way to browse collections, place orders, and have custom jewelry shipped worldwide.

CHAPTER FIVE
Practical Tips and Safety Information for Travelers in Corfu

To guarantee a safe and pleasurable vacation, it's critical to understand practical suggestions, emergency contacts, health measures, and the value of travel insurance. This book is intended to provide thorough information to help guests stay safe and make the most of their time in Corfu.

Staying Safe in Corfu

Emergency Contacts

1. Emergency Services: Dial 112 for police, fire, or medical assistance. Dial 100 for police problems, and 166 for medical situations.

2. Tourist Police: The Tourist Police in Corfu can be reached at +30 26610 88400. They are trained to assist tourists with various issues, including lost documents, thefts, and emergencies.

3. Embassy Contacts: Know the contact information for your country's embassy or consulate in Greece. They can provide assistance with passport issues, legal matters, and emergencies involving citizens abroad.

Health Precautions

1. Medical Facilities: Corfu has modern medical facilities, including hospitals, clinics, and pharmacies. In case of illness or injury, seek medical attention promptly. The General Hospital of Corfu is located in Corfu Town.

2. COVID-19 Precautions: Stay informed about current COVID-19 guidelines and restrictions in Corfu. Follow safety protocols such as wearing masks in public spaces, maintaining social distancing, and practicing good hygiene.

3. Travel Vaccinations: Check with your healthcare provider regarding recommended vaccinations or health precautions for traveling to Corfu. This may include vaccinations for hepatitis, tetanus, and other preventable diseases.

Travel Insurance

1. **Importance of Travel Insurance:** It's strongly recommended to have travel insurance that covers medical emergencies, trip cancellations, lost luggage, and other unforeseen circumstances.

Confirm that your insurance includes coverage for activities you plan to engage in, such as water sports or hiking.

2. Insurance Providers: Research reputable travel insurance providers and compare policies to find one that suits your needs. Ensure the policy covers emergency medical expenses, evacuation, and 24/7 assistance.

3. Documentation: Carry copies of your travel insurance policy, emergency contacts, and important documents such as passports, visas, and prescriptions. Store digital copies securely in case of loss or theft.

Local Laws and Customs

Respectful Behavior

1. Cultural Sensitivity: Familiarize yourself with local customs, traditions, and etiquette in Corfu. Respect religious sites, dress modestly when visiting churches or monasteries, and avoid public displays of affection in conservative areas.

2. Alcohol and Drugs: Adhere to legal drinking ages and consumption limits. Possession or use of illegal drugs is strictly prohibited and can result in severe penalties under Greek law.

3. Environmental Conservation: Respect natural environments, beaches, and protected areas. Dispose of waste responsibly, avoid littering, and support sustainable tourism practices.

Transportation Tips

Getting Around Safely

- Public Transport: Corfu provides public transportation alternatives including buses, taxis, and rental automobiles. Use trusted cab services and agree on fares before beginning your journey. When taking public transportation, follow all safety standards.
- Driving Precautions: Before hiring a car or scooter, review local traffic rules, road signs, and driving conditions. Drive carefully, especially on twisting coastal roads and through rural areas.
- Boat Safety: Prioritize safety when partaking in water activities or boat trips by wearing life jackets, following directions from guides or boat operators, and staying aware of weather conditions and sea currents.

Money and Valuables

Financial Security

1. Currency Exchange: Use authorized currency exchange services or withdraw money from ATMs located in secure locations. Be cautious of potential scams or unauthorized exchanges offering unrealistic rates.

2. Credit Cards: Use credit cards with chip technology for secure transactions. Inform your bank of your travel plans to avoid card blocks or fraud alerts while in Corfu.

3. Valuables Safety: Keep valuables such as passports, cash, jewelry, and electronics secure in hotel safes or locked compartments. Avoid carrying large amounts of cash or displaying expensive items in public.

Communication and Connectivity

Staying connected

1. Purchase a local SIM card for your phone to connect to local networks and data plans. This enables for more convenient communication, GPS navigation, and internet access while exploring Corfu.

2. Wi-Fi is widely available in Corfu's hotels, restaurants, and public locations for free. Use secure networks and avoid accessing critical information on public Wi-Fi networks.

3. Emergency Contacts List: Make a list of emergency contacts, including local authorities, hotel or lodging personnel, embassy/consulate contacts, and family members. Keep this information readily available in case of an emergency.

Weather and Outdoor Activities
Outdoor Safety

1. Weather Awareness: Corfu experiences a Mediterranean climate with hot summers and mild winters. Stay informed about weather forecasts, especially if engaging in outdoor activities such as hiking, swimming, or boating.

2. Sun Protection: Protect yourself from sun exposure by wearing sunscreen, sunglasses, hats, and lightweight clothing. Stay hydrated and seek shade during peak sun hours to avoid heat-related illnesses.

3. Natural Hazards: Be aware of potential natural hazards such as strong currents at beaches, rocky terrain on hiking trails, and wildlife encounters. Follow safety guidelines and heed warnings from local authorities.

Conclusion

Travelers who follow these practical recommendations and safety information can have a safe and happy stay in Corfu. These tips, which range from staying educated about emergency contacts and health precautions to practicing courteous behavior and protecting belongings, are intended to improve your travel experience and provide peace of mind while visiting this stunning island destination.

Local Laws and Etiquette
Tipping Guide

Tipping in Corfu is generally appreciated but not always expected. Here's a guide to tipping in various situations:

1. Restaurants and Cafés: If a service charge is not included, leaving a tip of around 5-10% of the total bill is customary. For exceptional service, you can round up or leave a slightly higher tip.

2. Hotels and Accommodations: It is customary to tip hotel employees who provide specialized services such as housekeeping, concierge help, and bellhop services. A daily gratuity of a few euros would be appreciated.

3. Tour Guides and Drivers: A gratuity of 5-10% of the tour fee or fare is usual, depending on the quality of service.

4. Spas and Salons: If you visit a spa or salon, tipping between 10-15% of the service cost is customary for exceptional treatment.

5. Taxis: Tipping taxi drivers is not required, however rounding up the fee or leaving a little gratuity is popular, especially for helpful or courteous drivers.

Dress Code:

Corfu's dress code is liberal, particularly in tourist regions and seaside resorts. However, it is courteous to dress appropriately in some contexts.

1. Dress modestly when visiting religious sites, such as churches and monasteries. Avoid shorts, sleeveless tops, and exposing apparel. Cover your shoulders and knees as a show of respect.

2. For luxury restaurants and formal events, dress smart casually or formally. Men can wear collared shirts and pants, and women can wear dresses or sophisticated ensembles.

3. Beachwear: While beachwear is suitable for beaches and pool areas, it's courteous to cover up when leaving these areas. Bring a cover-up, sarong, or lightweight clothing to wear when moving around public spaces.

4. Local Customs: Respect local customs and traditions regarding clothing. In rural areas or villages, dressing conservatively may be appreciated, especially when interacting with locals or attending cultural events.

Language Tips:

While Greek is the official language of Corfu, many residents, particularly in tourist areas, speak English effectively.

Here are some language guidelines for travelers.

1. Learn basic Greek language to enhance your vacation experience and appreciate the local culture. Phrases such as "hello" (Yassas), "thank you" (Efharisto), and "please" (Parakalo) are often used and warmly welcomed.

2. English availability: In tourist destinations, eateries, signs, and information are frequently available in English. However, making an attempt to speak a few Greek words is appreciated and can lead to pleasant exchanges with locals.

3. Use Translation or Language Learning Apps to improve communication. These apps might help you interpret menus and ask for directions or engaging in simple conversations.

4. Polite Gestures: Politeness and respectful gestures are universal. Saying "excuse me," smiling, and using polite tones go a long way in communication, even if language barriers exist.

Safety Tips and Precautions
General Safety

1. Awareness: Be mindful of your surroundings, especially in congested or tourist places.

Keep an eye on your possessions and don't overtly flaunt important items.

2. Night Safety: Corfu is typically safe at night, however it's recommended to stay in well-lit and busy locations. Use reliable transportation and avoid wandering alone in unfamiliar or remote regions.

3. Emergency Contacts: Keep emergency numbers for local police, medical services, and your embassy/consulate in case of emergency. Keep a copy of your travel insurance and critical documents secure.

Health precautions

1. Medical Facilities: Corfu offers excellent medical facilities and pharmacies. If you require medical attention, seek it from respected clinics or hospitals. Carry any necessary prescriptions as well as a first-aid kit.

2. Sun Protection: The Mediterranean sun can be intense. Wear sunscreen, sunglasses, and hats to protect yourself from sunburn and heat-related illnesses. Stay hydrated, especially during outdoor activities.

3. Water Safety: While tap water is generally safe in Corfu, consider drinking bottled water if you have a

sensitive stomach. Be cautious of strong currents and follow lifeguard instructions at beaches.

Transportation Safety

1. Use reliable public transit, such as buses or taxis. Confirm fares before beginning your trip, and be wary of any scams or overcharging.

2. Driving Tips: Before hiring a car or scooter, familiarize yourself with local traffic regulations and circumstances. Drive conservatively, particularly on curving roads or in rural areas.

3. Prioritize safety on boat tours and water activities by wearing life jackets, following guides' instructions, and staying alert of weather and sea currents.

Cultural insights and etiquette

Respectful behavior

1. Greetings! Greet residents with a warm "hello" (Yassas) or "good morning/afternoon/evening" (Kalimera/Kalispera/Kalinihta). Handshakes are usual in official contexts, but intimate friends and relatives may welcome with kisses on the cheek.

2. Respect elderly people by addressing them graciously and according to customary conventions, such as standing up or providing a seat.

3. Table Manners: Wait for the host to eat before starting your meal. Avoid resting your elbows on the table, and eat with utensils rather than your hands, unless it is usual for the meal.

Cultural sensitivity

1. Dress modestly and speak softly when visiting religious sites, including churches. Follow any explicit guidelines or restrictions governing behavior and photography on the property.

2. Personal Space: Greeks are known for their warmth and generosity, but they also value personal space and avoid intrusive questions or behaviors.

3. Gift Giving: When welcomed to someone's home, it is customary to bring a little gift, such as flowers, wine, or dessert. Avoid giving gifts with negative connotations, such as sharp objects or black-colored.

CHAPTER SIX
BONUS SECTION
Itineraries And Useful Greek Phrases to Use While Exploring Corfu

To make the most of your time on the island, you'll need well-planned itineraries and simple Greek Phrases. Itineraries ensures that you make the most of your time on this captivating island.

Sample Itineraries for Exploring Corfu

Corfu, with its captivating combination of history, natural beauty, and cultural legacy, provides a wide selection of experiences for visitors of all ages and interests. Whether you're looking for family-friendly activities, outdoor experiences, or cultural immersion, these sample itineraries will lead you on an unforgettable trip throughout the island.

3-Day Family Itinerary

Day 1: Discovering Corfu Town

- **Morning**: Explore Corfu's Old Town. The Old Fortress offers panoramic views of the city and the sea. Wander around the small streets, appreciate Venetian architecture, and see the Liston Promenade.

- **Afternoon**: Visit the Archaeological Museum of Corfu to discover ancient artifacts and history. Have a family lunch at a local taverna, trying traditional Greek dishes.
- **Evening**: Stroll along Spianada Square, enjoy street performances, and visit the Church of Saint Spyridon. End the day with dinner at a family-friendly restaurant.

Day 2: Beach Day and Water Activities

- **Morning**: Head to Glyfada Beach for a day of sun, sand, and water sports. Rent beach chairs and umbrellas for relaxation.
- **Afternoon**: Try water activities such as snorkeling, paddleboarding, or jet skiing. Have a picnic on the beach or enjoy beachside dining at a nearby taverna.
- **Evening**: Return to your accommodation for a relaxing evening by the pool or beach. Consider a family barbecue or seafood dinner.

Day 3: Nature and Adventure

- **Morning**: Visit Aqualand Corfu for a day of water park fun. Enjoy slides, wave pools, and attractions suitable for all ages.

- **Afternoon**: Explore the Corfu Trail or take a family-friendly hiking excursion in the countryside. Discover scenic viewpoints and natural landscapes.
- **Evening**: Have a farewell dinner at a family-friendly restaurant, savoring local specialties. Reflect on your Corfu adventures and plan future family trips.

5-Day Adventure Itinerary

Day 1: Coastal Exploration

- **Morning**: Start your adventure at Paleokastritsa Beach. Rent a kayak or take a boat tour to explore sea caves and hidden coves.
- **Afternoon**: Hike to Angelokastro, an ancient fortress with panoramic views. Enjoy a picnic lunch with scenic vistas.
- **Evening**: Return to your accommodation and relax by the beach or pool. Dine at a seaside restaurant for fresh seafood.

Day 2: Water Sports and Island Hopping

- **Morning**: Head to Kavos Beach for water sports activities such as windsurfing, parasailing, or jet boating.

- **Afternoon**: Take a boat excursion to nearby islands like Paxos or Antipaxos. Explore beaches, caves, and charming villages.
- **Evening**: Enjoy sunset cocktails at a beach bar or waterfront cafe. Experience the lively nightlife in Kavos if interested.

Day 3: Mountain Adventures

- **Morning**: Drive to Mount Pantokrator for hiking or mountain biking. Enjoy panoramic views of the island from the summit.
- **Afternoon**: Visit traditional villages like Pelekas or Lakones. Discover local culture, crafts, and scenic viewpoints.
- **Evening**: Have dinner at a mountain taverna, tasting traditional Greek dishes with mountainous flavors.

Day 4: Cultural Immersion

- **Morning**: Explore the Achilleion Palace, known for its historic architecture and gardens. Learn about Empress Elisabeth of Austria's legacy.
- **Afternoon**: Visit the Folklore Museum of Acharavi or the Museum of Asian Art in Corfu Town. Dive into the island's cultural heritage.

- **Evening**: Attend a Greek music and dance performance or cultural event. Enjoy a dinner with live music at a traditional taverna.

Day 5: Relaxation and Reflection

- **Morning**: Spend a relaxing morning at Agios Gordios Beach or Marathias Beach. Swim, sunbathe, or indulge in beachside yoga.
- **Afternoon**: Visit a local spa for wellness treatments and relaxation. Pamper yourself with massages or thermal baths.
- **Evening**: Reflect on your Corfu adventures with a farewell dinner at a seaside restaurant. Toast to memorable experiences and plan future travels.

7-Day Cultural Exploration

Day 1: Arrival in Corfu Town

- **Arrival**: Check into your accommodation in Corfu Town. Take a leisurely walk around the Old Town, admiring historic buildings and landmarks.
- **Evening**: Enjoy dinner at a traditional taverna, sampling local cuisine and specialties.

Day 2: Historical Landmarks

- **Morning**: Visit the Old Fortress and New Fortress for panoramic views and historical insights. Explore the Archaeological Museum of Corfu.
- **Afternoon**: Discover the Church of Saint Spyridon and the Palace of St. Michael and St. George. Wander through narrow streets and souvenir shops.
- **Evening**: Attend a cultural performance or concert in Corfu Town.

Day 3: Cultural Heritage

- **Morning**: Visit the Achilleion Palace, a tribute to Empress Elisabeth of Austria. Explore the palace gardens and exhibits.
- **Afternoon**: Tour the Byzantine Museum of Antivouniotissa and the Museum of Asian Art. Learn about Corfu's artistic and cultural influences.
- **Evening**: Dine at a traditional taverna with live music and authentic Greek flavors.

Day 4: Island Exploration

- **Morning**: Take a day trip to Paxos and Antipaxos islands. Explore beaches, caves, and scenic landscapes.

- **Afternoon**: Visit traditional villages like Lakones or Doukades. Experience local crafts, shops, and cafes.
- **Evening**: Enjoy sunset views and dinner at a seaside restaurant on Paxos or Antipaxos.

Day 5: Rural Experiences

- **Morning**: Drive to Mount Pantokrator for panoramic views and hiking trails. Visit mountain villages like Pelekas or Spartilas.
- **Afternoon**: Discover local wineries and olive groves. Take a wine tasting tour or olive oil tasting experience.
- **Evening**: Have dinner at a countryside taverna, savoring farm-to-table cuisine and regional specialties.

Day 6: Coastal Charm

- **Morning**: Spend a day at Paleokastritsa Beach. Enjoy water activities, boat tours, and relaxation by the sea.
- **Afternoon**: Visit Angelokastro, an ancient fortress with historical significance. Explore nearby caves and viewpoints.
- **Evening**: Return to Corfu Town for a farewell dinner at a waterfront restaurant.

Day 7: Departure and Reflection

- **Morning**: Explore Corfu Town for last-minute souvenirs and gifts. Visit local markets and artisan shops.
- **Afternoon**: Reflect on your Corfu journey and experiences. Write postcards or journal entries to capture memories.
- **Departure**: Transfer to the airport or port for departure. Depart with fond memories of Corfu and plans for future travels.

Here are 50 useful Greek phrases that travelers can use while exploring Corfu. These phrases cover greetings, common questions, and polite expressions to help you navigate and connect with the locals:

1. Good morning - Καλημέρα (Kaliméra)

2. Good evening - Καλησπέρα (Kalispéra)

3. Good night - Καληνύχτα (Kaliníhta)

4. Hello/Goodbye - Γειά σας (Yiásas)

5. Pleased to meet you - Χάρηκα πολύ (Hárika polí)

6. Yes - Ναι (Né)

7. No - Όχι (Óhi)

8. Thank you - Ευχαριστώ (Efcharistó)

9. You're welcome - Παρακαλώ (Parakaló)

10. Please - Παρακαλώ (Parakaló)

11. Okay/All right - Εντάξει (Endáxi)

12. Excuse me (to get attention) - Με συγχωρείτε (Me synchoríte)

13. Excuse me (to get past) - Συγγνώμη (Syngnómi)

14. Please write it down for me - Να μου το γράψετε, παρακαλώ; (Na mou to grápsete, parakaló?)

15. How are you? - Τι κάνετε; (Ti kánete?)

16. Fine, and you? - Καλά, εσείς; (Kalá, esís?)

17. Cheers/Your health! (when drinking) - Γειά μας! (Yiá mas!)

18. Could you help me? - Μπορείτε να με βοηθήσετε; (Boríte na me voithísete?)

19. Can you show me... - Μπορείτε να μου δείξετε... (Boríte na mou díxete...)

20. I want... - Θέλω... (Thélo...)

21. I don't know - Δεν ξέρω (Den xéro)

22. I don't understand - Δεν καταλαβαίνω (Den katalavéno)

23. Do you speak English? - Μιλάτε αγγλικά; (Miláte angliká?)

24. Can you please speak more slowly? - Μπορείτε να μιλήσετε πιο αργά, παρακαλώ; (Boríte na milísete pio argá, parakaló?)

25. Please say that again - Παρακαλώ, πείτε το ξανά (Parakaló, peíte to xaná)

26. Here   - Εδώ (Edó)

27. There   - Εκεί (Ekí)

28. What?   - Τι; (Ti?)

29. When?   - Πότε; (Póte?)

30. Why?   - Γιατί; (Giatí?)

31. Where?   - Πού; (Poú?)

32. How?   - Πώς; (Pós?)

33. I'm lost   - Έχω χαθεί (Écho chathí)

34. Can I have the menu, please?   - Μπορώ να έχω το μενού, παρακαλώ; (Boró na écho to menú, parakaló?)

35. The bill, please   - Τον λογαριασμό, παρακαλώ (Ton logariasmó, parakaló)

36. How much does it cost?   - Πόσο κοστίζει; (Póso kostízei?)

37. I would like...   - Θα ήθελα... (Tha íthela...)

38. Is there a bathroom here?   - Υπάρχει μπάνιο εδώ; (Ypárchei bánio edó?)

39. Help!   - Βοήθεια! (Voítheia!)

40. I'm allergic to...   - Έχω αλλεργία στο... (Écho allergía sto...)

41. I need a doctor   - Χρειάζομαι γιατρό (Chreiázomai giatró)

42. Call the police   - Καλέστε την αστυνομία (Kaléste tin astynomía)

43. I would like to buy... - Θα ήθελα να αγοράσω... (Tha íthela na agoráso...)

44. Do you have...? - Έχετε...; (Échete...?)

45. I like this - Αυτό μου αρέσει (Aftó mou arései)

46. It's too expensive - Είναι πολύ ακριβό (Eínai polý akrivó)

47. Can I try this on? - Μπορώ να το δοκιμάσω; (Boró na to dokimáso?)

48. What time is it? - Τι ώρα είναι; (Ti óra eínai?)

49. I'm here on vacation - Είμαι εδώ για διακοπές (Eímai edó gia diakopés)

50. I love Corfu! - Αγαπώ την Κέρκυρα! (Agapó tin Kérkyra!)

These phrases should help you communicate basic needs and socialize with the locals. Enjoy your travels in Corfu!.

CHAPTER SEVEN

Capturing the Beauty of Corfu: Stunning Photos of Landscapes, Historical Sites, and Culinary Delights

Corfu, provides a visual feast for both photographers and travelers. From spectacular scenery and historic ruins to delectable culinary delights, every area of the island offers opportunities to shoot amazing images that tell the narrative of Corfu's attraction and charm.

Landscapes and seascapes

Corfu's landscapes are a beautiful combination of azure waters, lush hillsides, and attractive villages. Here are some breathtaking images that capture the island's natural beauty:

1. Sunset over Paleokastritsa.

A golden sunset over Paleokastritsa Beach creates a beautiful sight, with boat silhouettes against the backdrop of the Ionian Sea.

2. Olive grove in spring

The rich foliage of an olive grove in April, with sunlight pouring through the branches, exemplifies Corfu's agricultural legacy and natural bounty.

3. Azure Waters of Agios Gordios.

The crystal-clear waters of Agios Gordios Beach enable people to swim, snorkel, and enjoy the beauty of Corfu's coastline, which is bordered by cliffs and rocky formations.

4. Mountain View from Mount Pantokrator.

A panoramic view from Mount Pantokrator shows the island's various geography, from rough mountains to verdant valleys, delivering a taste of Corfu's natural marvels.

Historic Sites

Corfu's rich past is evident in its historic ruins, fortifications, and architectural marvels. Here are breathtaking photographs of the island's historical sites:

1. Achilleion Palace Gardens

The beautiful gardens of Achilleion Palace, complete with statues and fountains, transport visitors to a bygone era of imperial grandeur and classical grace.

2. The Old Fortress of Corfu Town

The magnificent walls and battlements of Corfu Town's Old Fortress, which overlooks the sea, are a tribute to the island's historical strategic importance.

3. The Ancient Ruins of Palaiopolis

The archeological site of Palaiopolis exhibits vestiges of ancient civilizations, including temples, walls, and constructions that speak of Corfu's former splendor.

4. Monrepos Estate Gardens

The serene gardens of Mon Repos Estate, surrounded by lush greenery and overlooking the sea, offer a peaceful retreat and historical insights into Corfu's aristocratic heritage.

Culinary Delights

Corfu's cuisine is a delicious blend of Greek flavors, fresh seafood, and Mediterranean ingredients. Here are breathtaking photographs of the island's culinary delights:

1. Seafood Platter in a Taverna

A colorful seafood platter in a seaside taverna, which includes grilled fish, calamari, shrimp, and octopus, exemplifies Corfu's coastal gastronomy and culinary traditions.

2. Traditional Greek Meze Selection.

A delicious selection of classic Greek meze dishes, such as tz atziki, grilled halloumi, filled vine leaves, and olives, exemplifies Corfu's culinary richness and freshness.

5. Greek desserts and pastries.

A enticing array of Greek desserts and pastries, such as baklava, loukoumades, and galaktoboureko, displays Corfu's sweet tooth and fondness for Mediterranean delicacies.

Conclusion

These stunning photos of Corfu's landscape, historical buildings, and gastronomic delights take us on a visual trip that encapsulates the soul and beauty of the island. Corfu's visual attraction, from turquoise seascapes and ancient ruins to delectable cuisine and cultural events, invites you to explore, savor, and treasure your memories of this wonderful Greek island.

As the sun sets below the horizon, throwing a golden glow across the Ionian Sea, we conclude our excursion over the picturesque island of Corfu. This travel guide is a labor of love, a tapestry of history, culture, and natural beauty woven together to help you discover the essence of this Greek paradise. Corfu, with its beautiful hills, turquoise waters, and timeless elegance of the Old Town, has provided us with a wealth of adventures. We've traveled through olive fields, sampled the local kumquat liqueur, and participated in traditional panegyric. We've visited Byzantine fortresses, marveled at French and British architecture, and felt the Venetian romance in the air.

As tourists, we want to feel the places we visit, to become part of their story, even if only for a brief period. Corfu has allowed us to do exactly that: write our own stories on its sandy beaches and beneath its old fortifications. We've discovered that Corfu is more than just a place; it's a mood, a state of mind in which history, nature, and hospitality combine effortlessly. In this book, we've covered everything from must-see attractions to secret jewels known only to locals. We've included practical tips for getting around, remaining safe, and making the most of your time on the island. More than that, we tried to capture the essence of Corfu, giving you a sense of its rhythm and heartbeat.

As you finish this book, remember that every end is merely a new beginning. The stories you've read have become a part of you, urging you to embark on your adventure, to discover your route across Corfu's rich landscapes. Whether you seek solace in the stillness of a mountain village or the thrill of a summer festival, Corfu is a destination that will stay with you, leaving a memory not only in images but also in your soul.

So pack your bags, bring your sense of adventure, and set off for Corfu. The island greets you with open arms, eager to disclose its secrets and become a part of your travel stories. And when you're there, standing on a rock with the sea breeze in your hair, remember this guide, your faithful companion on the journey to discovering one of Greece's most precious jewels.

Thank you for choosing this guide as your gateway to Corfu. May your travels be safe, your experiences rich, and your memories everlasting. Until we meet again, Καλό ταξίδι (safe travels) and Αντίο (farewell), dear reader.

Printed in Great Britain
by Amazon

45916408R00143